KW-242-208

Covenants for Title
Understanding the New Law

Professor Phillip H. Kenny
LLB, Dip Crim LLM, Solicitor

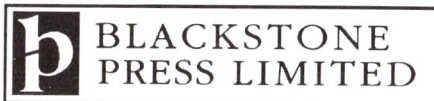

BLACKSTONE
PRESS LIMITED

First published in Great Britain 1995 by Blackstone Press Limited, 9–15 Aldine Street, London W12 8AW. Telephone 0181-740 1173

© P. H. Kenny, 1995

ISBN: 1 85431 471 8

British Library Cataloguing in Publication Data
A CIP catalogue record for this book is available from the British Library

UNIVERSITY OF PLYMOUTH
LIBRARY SERVICES

UNIVE   ...   JTH

Item No.	9 00 2 4 4 3 5 5 3
Date	1 2 OCT 1995 B
Class No.	340·0438 KEN
Contl. No.	1854314718

LIBRARY SERVICES

Typeset by Montage Studios Limited, Tonbridge, Kent
Printed by Ashford Colour Press, Gosport, Hampshire

All rights reserved. No part of this book may be reproduced or transmitted in any form or by any means, electronic or mechanical, including photocopying, recording, or any information storage or retrieval system without prior permission from the publisher.

WITHDRAWN
FROM
UNIVERSITY OF PLYMOUTH
LIBRARY SERVICES

90 0244355 3

Covenants for Title
Understanding the New Law

SEVEN DAY LOAN

This book is to be returned on
or before the date stamped below

16 FEB 1998
CANCELLED

INTER-SITE LOAN
Exc

CANCELLED
1 8 MAR 1998

2·8·99

28/9/99.

1 3 MAY 2004

UNIVERSITY OF PLYMOUTH

PLYMOUTH LIBRARY

Tel: (01752) 232323
This book is subject to recall if required by another reader
Books may be renewed by phone
CHARGES WILL BE MADE FOR OVERDUE BOOKS

Contents

When are the statutory covenants implied? — Covenant concerning the right to dispose and for further assurance — Covenant for
freedom from encumbrances — Freedom from encumbrances –
full title guarantee — What are 'charges and encumbrances' and
'all other rights exercisable by third parties'? — Miscellaneous
statutory rights — Freedom from encumbrances – limited title
guarantee — Covenants relating to leasehold land — Further
leasehold covenant (s. 4) — Further covenant where there is a
mortgage of leasehold land or land subject to a rentcharge (s. 5)
— Limited effect of covenants (s. 6) — Passing the benefit of
covenants (s. 7) — Welsh form of covenant (s. 8(4)) —
Construction of covenants (s. 8(2)) — Transitional provisions

The position where no covenant for title is given — Should a seller
be unwilling to give a full title guarantee? — The relevance of the

Standard Conditions of Sale — Patent defects in title — Relevance of other remedies — Summary of the no-covenant position — The position of mortgagees — Covenants for title in registered land — Covenants for title and particular conveyancing parties — Covenants for title under particular statutes

Preface

Part I of the Law of Property (Miscellaneous Provisions) Act 1994 comes into force on 1 July 1995. It is the work of the Law Commission. It must be said it is largely seen as unwelcome and unnecessary by conveyancers and will pass unnoticed by the lay person. The purpose of this book is to assist practitioners in coming to terms with the Act and throw some light on the darker corners of this legislation. Conscious of the fact that the younger half of the profession have qualified at a time when formal teaching of covenants for title has been omitted almost entirely from the curriculum I have strayed sometimes far into statements that to many will be self-evident. Conscious of the heated debate that will occur in the next year or so over the application of these covenants I have sometimes strayed into areas that some may see as fanciful. I have tried in the main to steer a middle course between these two extremes of presentation. The Act, though brief by our very lamentable contemporary standards, contains much food for thought and I hope I assist in its digestion.

Phillip H. Kenny
20 June 1995

Table of Cases

Table of Statutes

Page numbers in **bold** refer to quoted text.

Table of Statutes

1

The Basic Scheme

The regime of covenants for title which is known to conveyancers today dates from the Conveyancing Act 1887. In the Law of Property Act 1925 amendments were made and the new covenants for title were set out in sch. 2 to that Act where they lay largely undisturbed for 70 years.

The Law Commission thought the topic a proper one for reform and discussed it in Working Paper No. 107, *Transfer of Land: Implied Covenants for Title*. Legislation was proposed in a report (Law Com. No. 199). The Bill itself was the first to be considered using the Jellicoe procedure for law reform Bills. The proceedings of the special standing committee are published as HL Paper 62 (Session 1993–4). However, this is of limited assistance because later amendments were made to the Bill (House of Lords 20 June 1994). The Bill became the Law of Property (Miscellaneous Provisions) Act 1994 which was given royal assent on 3 November 1994 and was brought into force on 1 July 1995.

Since 1925 there have been less than a handful of reported cases in which covenants for title have been in issue. Indeed, in the case of registered land there are virtually none. Is this a remarkable tribute to the skill of the drafters of the 1925 legislation or to the irrelevance of the covenants for title?

It is certainly not the former because, as the Law Commission was able to demonstrate, and was anyway perfectly well known to conveyancers, there were problems with the system of covenants for title set up by the Law of Property Act 1925, sch. 2.

As the number of conveyancing transactions has increased so vastly over the years, and not without a considerable increase in conveyancing-related litigation, why have disputes relating to covenants for title not proliferated? Many factors have contributed to this. First the covenants for title provide a fairly clearly understood statement of last resort of the obligations of the seller after completion. Secondly conveyancing is carried out by professionals who overwhelmingly prefer to cooperate to sort out problems. Thirdly there has been a growth in the availability of other remedies after completion — the law of misrepresentation particularly covers some of the same ground as the covenants for title. Finally the accelerating spread of registration of title has and will continue to reduce the scope for uncertainty in conveyancing titles.

Against this rather comfortable background, why did the Law Commission believe, and Parliament agree, that *reform* of the law of implied covenants was in the public interest or necessary? The justifications given are in terms of clearness, certainty and accessibility by the consumer. This book as a whole will examine whether the new legislation is clear and certain from the lawyer's point of view. The question of comprehensibility by the consumer can be dealt with here. The writer has long believed that achieving easy comprehensibility by the law consumer is not a sensible aim for legislation in the modern complex world. Least of all can it be achieved in an area so technical as that concerned with the covenants for title to real property. It is a case of tinkering. Tinkering with a vast and creaking edifice. The lay person is far from having a realistic chance of understanding the whole, let alone the effect of 12 sections of technical tinkering.

So much for the significance of the legislation for the lay person. The past few decades have not involved much heated debate among solicitors about covenants for title. Because the pattern of covenants to be given in different conveyancing situations has become routine, some conveyancers may assume that beneficial owners are bound in law to give the beneficial owner covenant and so on. In reality no covenant is required at all except in a very small proportion of cases where they are prescribed by statute. The theory is that covenants for title are negotiated between the parties, and this theory is given practical effect by the new Act.

This is then the immediate practical result of this small piece of law reform. Old dogs must learn new tricks. In almost every case the particular covenant for title to be given must be agreed between the parties. There will inevitably be discussions, disagreement and even heated debate. An educated guess may be that in a year or two's time the pattern of covenants to be given in particular transactions will be as clear as in the golden conveyancing days of my youth. Until then solicitors will have to give thought to which form of words to use in each transaction and some effort to understanding their effect. In negotiations, information and comprehension are strong tools and it is hoped the reader will find in these pages some assistance in their forging.

The new law reduces the number of statutory covenants for title. There are now only two. These are a covenant with full title guarantee and a covenant with limited title guarantee. This gives the drafter five alternatives. The document may be drafted with no covenants for title at all, with one of the two statutory covenants for title, or with some variation of the statutory covenants for title, or with some tailor-made covenant for title.

In reality the last of these alternatives is of very limited value. The statutory covenants for title run with the land benefited, formerly by virtue of the Law of Property Act 1925, s. 76(6), and in future by s. 7 of the 1994 Act. But covenants other than the statutory covenants are not covered by s. 7 and the benefit of them will not run with the land. In consequence any die-hard who devoutly wishes to continue with old covenants for title or some version thereof will be encouraged to desist.

The writer's own view is that by and large the simple scheme proposed in the legislation should be followed in conveyancing practice. The writer would, therefore, follow the scheme suggested in the following table:

Conveyance by	Covenants to be given
Beneficial owner(s)	With full title guarantee.
By surviving joint tenant	With full title guarantee (and a recital of benefical entitlement is now required to gain the benefit of the Law of Property (Joint Tenants) Act 1964).
Landlord under the Leasehold Reform Act 1967	With limited title guarantee.
Landlord under the Housing Act 1985	With full title guarantee.
Landlord under the Leasehold Reform, Housing and Urban Development Act 1993	With limited title guarantee.
All other estate owners and conveyancing parties except settlors and donors	With limited title guarantee.
Settlor or donor	Convey as settlor or donor and no covenant is implied or (with limited title guarantee if willing to do so).

In this table the last entry can be in no doubt. A donor need give no promise as to the title conveyed and the donee is in no position to extract one. As will be explained below the three statutory cases are also unarguable.

Another very strong view has been given as to how solicitors should respond to the Act. This would suggest a quite different pattern of behaviour from that proposed in the above table. In evidence on the Bill, Mr Nugee (HL Paper 62, p. 49) said that in his view the legislation was:

(a) senseless, (b) likely to add to the complication of conveyancing, in relation to both registered and unregistered land, (c) unfair and (d) likely to lead to an increase in litigation, or at any rate in the complication of litigation.

At p. 50 he said further:

> I have no doubt that any solicitor who allows his client to convey land 'with full guarantee' will be liable for negligence, in the event of a defect in title appearing for which the vendor would not have been liable under the present beneficial owner covenants but for which he is liable under the new form of covenant.

In any negligence case that arises from the covenants for title Mr Nugee's view will be of interest to the court. The writer's own view is that the solicitor's position will depend very much on what the 'surprise encumbrance' is which is covered by the new covenant for title but not the old. Is it one which a reasonably competent solicitor would have discovered or should have foreseen? Even though negligence law has developed in recent years it does not make the solicitor a guarantor of his or her client's affairs. A reasonably competent vendor solicitor will investigate title accordingly. There is no reason to expect that the consequence Mr Nugee suggests will automatically follow.

2

The Legislation Described

When are the statutory covenants implied?

The statutory covenants set out in the 1994 Act are implied if a disposition of property is effected (actually or purportedly) by an instrument and the disposition is expressed to be made either 'with full title guarantee' or 'with limited title guarantee'.

Disposition

Section 1(4) of the Act states that 'disposition' includes the creation of a term of years, so the range of dispositions into which the statutory covenants may be implied is very wide. If the statutory formulae are used then covenants can be implied into, for example, gifts, leases, tenancy agreements, assignments of leases, mortgages, options, contracts for sale or other dispositions. Under the pre-1995 law it was important to know whether the disposition was for valuable consideration or not. Under the new law that is not so: the implication of the new covenants simply depends on whether or not the correct introductory words are used.

Instrument

The statutory covenants can be implied only when a disposition is effected by an instrument, and, by s. 1(4), 'instrument' includes an instrument which is not a deed. It may, thus, be a contract. The minimum requirement is probably writing. The conveyancing transactions into which the covenants cannot be implied because there is no instrument are those effected orally. In practical terms that is only leases falling within the Law of Property Act 1925, s. 54(2), namely, leases taking effect in possession for a term not exceeding three years at the best rent which can reasonably be obtained without a premium. It is suggested in *Current Law Statutes Annotated* that the covenants may not be implied in an equitable underlease but there is no good reason for this curious view since 'instrument' can include any form of contract.

Consideration

Section 1(1) specifically provides that the covenants can be implied in instruments which are not dispositions for valuable consideration. Whether any conveyancer will choose to imply covenants into instruments without consideration is considered at page 47.

Property

The Act is not confined to dispositions of real property. Section 1(1) refers to a 'disposition of property' and s. 1(4) states:

'property' includes a thing in action, and any interest in real or personal property.

The new terms of covenants for title can, thus, be used in a wide range of documents outside conveyancing provided the correct words are used to introduce them. This has potential in transactions such as sales and acquisitions of companies and sales of chattels. The buyer will presumably argue fiercely that the contract should be made with the statutory title guarantee and this will be resisted as always by the seller. There is potential for the new words to replace much of the ground presently covered by title warranties. As already indicated the clear potential of the legislation is to create disputes between lawyers.

Dispositions which are outside the Act

As has been seen the new covenants for title cannot be implied into dispositions which are not effected by an instrument. Neither can these covenants for title be implied if no real or personal property is disposed of. Thus, the statutory covenants cannot be implied into a grant of a licence. Despite curious views expressed from time to time by academic lawyers there is no doubt that a licence is not an instrument under which property as such passes. If an instrument which is in law a licence states that the licensor grants the licence, with full title guarantee, then the effect is as follows. The guarantees implied by s. 1 of the Act are not on the face of it implied because there is no purported disposition of an interest in property. A licence is not an interest in property at all. What effect will the court then give to the words purporting to guarantee the licensor's title? If included in any instrument produced by a lawyer in the future it is the obvious inference that the words (not hitherto used in conveyancing documents) are intended to introduce the promises contained in the 1994 Act. It is suggested here that the court must give the words the meaning they were so obviously intended to have. So far as they are relevant to the transaction in question the promises implied by the Act will be implied into any document in which they are used *whether or not that document falls within the ambit of s. 1 of the Act.*

If this serendipitous result does follow, the covenants implied will not have quite the effect which they have when implied into instruments which do fall within the Act. Most obviously s. 7 of the Act (see page 26 below) cannot apply in a case where there is no disposition of property. Section 7 provides for the benefit of the covenant to run with the land disposed of but by definition no land is disposed of by a licence which creates only personal rights.

Covenant concerning the right to dispose and for further assurance

This set of promises is contained in s. 2 of the Act. It applies where the disposition is expressed to be made with either full title guarantee or limited title guarantee. It has the following aspects:

    (1)   ... covenants—
        (a)   that the person making the disposition has the right (with the concurrence of any other person conveying the property) to dispose of the property as he purports to, and

(b) that that person will at his own cost do all that he reasonably can to give the person to whom he disposes of the property the title he purports to give.

(2) The latter obligation includes—

(a) in relation to a disposition of an interest in land the title to which is registered, doing all that he reasonably can to ensure that the person to whom the disposition is made is entitled to be registered as proprietor with at least the class of title registered immediately before the disposition; and

(b) in relation to a disposition of an interest in land the title to which is required to be registered by virtue of the disposition, giving all reasonable assistance fully to establish to the satisfaction of the Chief Land Registrar the right of the person to whom the disposition is made to registration as proprietor.

Right to dispose (s. 2(1)(a))

There is a breach of this covenant if the covenantor does not have the right to convey either the interest in or the physical property to which the conveyance *purports* to apply.

Examples of a breach of this promise would be:

(a) Land described in the conveyance is not in the seller's title. An example from the pre-1995 law is found in *A. J. Dunning and Sons (Shopfitters) Ltd* v *Sykes and Son (Poole) Ltd* [1987] Ch 287, CA. The transfer by the seller included a strip of land which, at the time of the transfer, was no longer within the seller's registered title because it had previously been sold to another purchaser. This was held to be a breach of the covenant for title. Under the pre-1995 law there was liability for breach of the covenant for 'good right to convey' only if the purchaser had had some title and that was so in this case. The rule was put clearly in *Barnsley's Conveyancing Law and Practice*, 3rd ed. (London: Butterworths, 1988), p. 603:

A purchaser cannot, therefore, sue his vendor on the covenant if the vendor's interest ceased before completion (otherwise than as a result of his own act or default), or even if he never had any title at all. Thus, a vendor will incur no liability under the statutory covenants where the conveyance includes land which never belonged to him or his predecessors in title but is vested in an adjacent owner under an independent title, or land wrongly occupied by the vendor and in respect of which no title has been acquired by adverse possession.

That is no longer the rule under the covenant given by s. 2 of the 1994 Act. The covenant in s. 2 *for good right to convey* means precisely what it says and covers cases where the seller has no title now and has never had title. A practical difficulty is discussed further below. There is in such a case no land to which the benefit of the covenant can attach and, thus, if the purchaser purports to resell then the second purchaser will not have the benefit of the covenant given by the original seller (see the discussion of s. 7 at page 26).

(b)   The seller has lost, e.g., by limitation, the title to land described in the conveyance — see, e.g., *Eastwood* v *Ashton* [1915] AC 900.

(c)   The seller does not have sufficient title to grant the freehold or leasehold interest purported to be conveyed. Thus, a lessee who grants a lease longer than his existing lease and does so with full or limited title guarantee would be in breach of this covenant for title.

The words in parentheses in s. 2(1)(a) — 'with the concurrence of any other person conveying the property' — seem to apply only where there is a joint disposition. They allow for the fact that each joint disponor only has a right to dispose if the other or others concur.

If a disposition requires the agreement of another person who is not joining in making the disposition, and it has not been expressly made subject to that agreement, then the disponor will be purporting to make the disposition as if agreement had been obtained and will be in breach of the s. 2(1)(a) covenant if it is not obtained. It is not enough for the disponor to be in a position to compel consent: the covenant requires the disponor to take the necessary steps to obtain the consent and to bear the cost of so doing.

For example, if consent is required for a conveyance made under a trust for sale (such consent not being dispensed with by the Law of Property

Act 1925, s. 2) then failure to obtain the consent will be in breach of the s. 2(1)(a) covenant because the disponor is not entitled to dispose of the land 'as he purports to', that is, without the required consent.

Where consent by a landlord or superior lessee is required to the assignment of a lease and is not obtained there will not be a breach of this covenant. That is because the assignment as such is effective without the consent. There may, though, be a breach of the covenant given by s. 4 of this Act (see page 23 below).

The words 'as he purports to' in s. 2(1)(a) refer to the subject-matter and manner of the disposition. If the person making the disposition purports to make it in a particular capacity but in fact is not able to make the disposition in that capacity then the covenant in s. 2(1)(a) is breached even if the person could convey in another capacity. For example, if a disposition is expressed to be made of the disponor's own property when in fact the disponor is acting for another under a power of attorney then there is a breach of s. 2(1)(a).

Further assurance (s. 2(1)(b))

This is likely to be one of the most fought-over parts of the legislation. The wording is straightforward but very hard to apply in practice. What is it reasonable for a seller to do at his own cost to put the title right?

Suppose a strip of land is lost to the title by adverse possession — is it reasonable to require the seller's own money to be used to acquire the title from the adverse possessor? Eventually the court may have to decide issues such as:

(a) Is the test of what is reasonable entirely objective?

(b) Is the lack of capacity of the seller of any relevance? After failing to convey the property title the seller may become insane or die. Clearly his or her receiver or executor may be *able* to take the necessary steps but will they have to? The problem arises because there are no steps to be taken by the seller personally. Presumably the words 'will ... do all that he reasonably can' will be applied to those who represent the now incapable convenantor.

A further potential for disagreement lies in this. A step may be reasonably feasible but very expensive. Does the concept of reasonableness in s. 2(1)(b) involve only the feasibility of a task or the cost which the seller is obliged to incur? Although the paragraph is unclear on this point the latter is the only sensible construction. In practice the court might be led to limiting the cost which it is reasonable to incur to the damages which the purchaser could expect to obtain if the defect was not corrected.

Obligation to assist with registration of title

Section 2(2) applies specifically to dispositions of interests in land and adds some detail to the promise for further assurance contained in s. 2(1)(b). It is in two parts. Paragraph (a) applies where title to the land is already registered. Paragraph (b) applies where the title will have to be registered by virtue of the disposition.

Section 2(2)(a) applies where the title is already registered. All must be done that the seller reasonably can do to ensure that the purchaser is *entitled* to be registered with at least the same class of title. In practical terms this adds very little to the promise for further assurance. The Land Registry generally expresses no unwillingness where land is registered to continue registration with at least the same class of title.

The provision may have particular relevance in cases where the land is registered but the seller is not the registered proprietor. This occurs when the seller has gained the right to sell by transmission, gift or subcontract. Also where the seller is selling under a power given by the proprietor and when selling as mortgagee. In each of these cases the seller will have to provide particular documents or evidence to the Land Registry if the purchaser is to obtain registration. Section 2(2)(a) specifically requires the seller to produce that evidence where it is reasonable to do so at the seller's own cost. It is also clear that this obligation and the one in s. 2(2)(b) apply whether or not the Land Registry is correct in its view that further evidence of the title is required. For example, the seller may have a title (based on length of possession and notoriety of that possession) which any reasonable buyer would accept but the Land Registry may insist unhelpfully on further evidence. The implied covenant for title requires the seller's assistance with even an otiose Land Registry requisition.

Section 2(2)(b) deals with situations where compulsory registration of title follows a disposition. It requires the seller to give reasonable assistance (again at the seller's own cost) to establish the right of the buyer to be registered as proprietor. It will be noted that s. 2(2)(b) does not specify with which title the purchaser has to be established as proprietor.

Thus, a seller may offer a documentary title which a buyer accepts. In due course the Land Registry (taking an unusually unhelpful line) may offer only a possessory title. This does not appear to be a breach of s. 2(1) or of s. 2(2). The promise given by s. 2(2)(b) is considerably weakened in cases where the Land Registry will permit registration but only with a lesser title. This potential weakness in the covenant can be avoided by a purposive construction of the basic promise given by s. 2(1)(b). What is the title which the seller 'purports to give'? That is considered next.

The title which the seller 'purports to give'

This replaces the expression in the previous legislation — 'as regards the subject-matter or share of subject-matter *expressed* to be conveyed by him' (Law of Property Act 1925, s. 76(1), emphasis added). The meaning of these words was considered in *May* v *Platt* [1900] 1 Ch 616 and in *George Wimpey and Co. Ltd* v *Sohn* [1967] Ch 487. So far as the new words are concerned it can be argued that if the covenantor purports to give a *fee simple* title then the equivalent registration is absolute title. The expression 'fee simple' in the conveyance if unregistered cannot refer to registered titles which are qualified to inferior forms of the title absolute. The same argument, though less cogently, would suggest that an *unqualified* grant of a leasehold estate should lead to registration with leasehold title absolute. So far as the fee simple is concerned this construction is necessary to give any worthwhile meaning to s. 2(2)(b). So far as leasehold titles are concerned the inclusion or variation of SCS 8.2.4 (2nd ed.); 3.2.2 or 3.2.3 (3rd ed.) (discussed below) will generally make the position clear.

The argument put forward here that the registered title which the seller purports to confer will be a fee simple absolute is suggested by an important general principle of conveyancing law. Where no statement as to the title or interest to be sold is included in a contract it is implied that the sale is of an unencumbered freehold (see, e.g., *Timmins* v *Moreland Street Property Co. Ltd* [1958] Ch 110). If there is nothing to rebut this in the contract then that should be the title which the seller 'purports to give'. There is no similar presumption on the grant of a lease. However, the landlord clearly purports to grant a lease — should this not also imply that it is a secure unencumbered lease to which title absolute will be granted? (Some support to this view is given by *Becker* v *Partridge* [1966] 2 QB 155.)

Presumption about the title disposed of

Section 2(3) applies where the seller sells an existing legal interest in land. It thus does not apply on the grant of a lease. There is a presumption if the title is registered that the disposition is of the whole of that interest (s. 2(3)(a)). If the title is not registered then there are two presumptions:

(a) If the interest is leasehold, that the disposition is for the unexpired term of the lease (s. 2(3)(b)(i)).
(b) In any other case, that the fee simple is disposed of (s. 2(3)(b)(ii)).

Section 2(3) as a whole also seems very limited in its practical impact. The presumptions it contains are 'subject to the terms of the instrument'. If normal conveyancing procedure is followed the instrument itself will make implicit the interest which is disposed of.

If the contract for a disposition does make it clear that a limited interest is intended but the terms of the instrument do not there will be no inadvertent practical effect from s. 2(3). The remedy of rectification should be available to ensure that the instrument is given effect to in the way intended by the contract.

Covenant for freedom from encumbrances

The promise as to freedom from encumbrances is contained in s. 3 of
the Act. There are separate provisions where the full title guarantee is
given and where the limited title guarantee is given.

Freedom from encumbrances — full title guarantee

If a disposition is expressed to be made with full title guarantee, the
basic promise is contained in s. 3(1). The covenant is that the property
is disposed of free:

(a)   from all charges and encumbrances (whether monetary or
not), and
(b)   from all other rights exercisable by third parties,
other than any charges, encumbrances or rights which that person
[i.e., the person making the disposition] does not and could not
reasonably be expected to know about.

Before analysing this very sweeping provision it is helpful to look at
s. 3(2) which provides some clarification by making it clear that the
charges etc. coming within s. 3(1) can include liabilities and rights
conferred by an enactment. It then states that certain rights and liabilities
conferred by enactments are not charges etc. within s. 3(1). These are
liabilities and rights which are 'not such as to constitute defects in title'
because they are only:

(a)   potential liabilities and rights in relation to the property, or
(b)   liabilities and rights imposed or conferred in relation to property
generally.

Examples of the former could be the possibility of rights being granted
to statutory undertakers under the Gas, Water or Electricity Acts. Each
of the Gas Act 1986, The Water Industry Act 1991 and Electricity Act
1989 contain powers for various rights in the nature of easements to be
created in favour of the suppliers of those services. Clearly when
granted these would be rights exercisable by third parties and, thus,
within s. 3(1)(b). Their possibility would, though *at the time of the*

15

disposition still be only potential rights and so would not amount to a breach of the promise made by s. 3(1).

Examples of things falling under (b) are the State ownership of radioactive minerals; the liability to pay any property taxes imposed for the time being or obligations to comply with environmental legislation.

What are 'charges and encumbrances' and 'all other rights exercisable by third parties'?

Charges

Technically in property law a mortgage and a charge may be different things. The former involves a transfer of property rights while the latter does not. There are a variety of names for such rights — mortgages, charges by way of legal mortgage, equitable charges and liens. Any attempt to define each of these in the context of this legislation is pointless. If the court were constrained to look at a technical definition of charge — which might exclude both mortgages and liens — no consequence would follow. The covenantor's promise is to sell free of all the things mentioned in s. 3(1). If the property is subject to a mortgage, charge or lien of any kind then there is a breach of s. 3(1). Whether that is because the right to which the property is subject is a charge or encumbrance or any 'other right' makes not one jot of difference.

Encumbrances

For the reason given in the note on charges it is not necessary to waste any effort on defining encumbrances. Because if the court were to take a restrictive view of the meaning of this term then the claim in question would be tested by whether it falls within s. 3(1)(b) as 'other rights'. Anything which could be a charge or an encumbrance from which the property is not free must be a right exercisable by a third party. In consequence it is to the meaning of this last term that our attention must turn.

Other rights exercisable by third parties

This is a novel expression. As the sweeping-up provision in s. 3(1) it gives meaning to the whole. It is possible that the expression will be construed in the light of *National Provincial Bank Ltd* v *Ainsworth* [1965] AC 1175 in which the meaning of the word 'right' in the Land Registration Act 1925, s. 70(1)(g), was considered. Lord Wilberforce would not give that expression its plain English meaning but said, at pp. 1247–8:

> Before a right or interest can be admitted into the category of property, or of a right affecting property, it must be definable, identifiable by third parties, capable in its nature of assumption by third parties, and have some degree of permanence or stability.

Whether this view is taken of 'rights' under the present Act cannot of course be predicted for certain. The Act was allegedly recommended by the Law Commission in order to state this area of law in language which could be understood by the lay person. This is not a claim that ever could be made on behalf of Lord Wilberforce. Some examples will illustrate the difficulty involved.

Chivers and Sons Ltd v *Air Ministry* [1955] Ch 585 This case involved liability for chancel repairs. Under the law before the 1994 Act this did not come within the covenant for freedom from encumbrances because it was not made, occasioned or suffered by the seller. This will now clearly be a right within s. 3(1) of the 1994 Act.

A neighbour claims the right to enter on the land to abate a nuisance If proved this is definitely in plain English a right exercisable by a third party. It is not, however, a right in property law strictly within *National Provincial Bank Ltd* v *Ainsworth*. There is, too, a possibility of this being only a 'potential liability' within s. 3(2)(b) and in consequence not within the scope of the s. 3(1) covenant.

Egg v *Blayney* (1888) 21 QBD 107 This case involved charges for street paving which were the liability of the owner for the time being of the property. Under the old law these charges were not an encumbrance.

17

This is in contrast with road charges which were held to be a charge on the property and consequently an encumbrance in *Stock* v *Meakin* [1900] 1 Ch 683. Again in common English both these charges would be rights exercisable by third parties. The former, however, is not a property right in the sense discussed.

Miscellaneous statutory rights

There is a very great range of statutory rights which are not within the exception to s. 3 as applying to property generally but apply to particular property. These matters arising under planning legislation, housing legislation and so on, and may give rise to 'rights exercisably by third parties' in the plain literal sense of these words. Again a restricted view of the term 'rights' is necessary to exclude these matters from the scope of the covenants for title. But, why should such a restrictive view be taken? Thus, the new legislation may bring within the scope of the covenants for title matters such as listed building orders, and tree preservation orders. The potential effect of such an interpretation is reduced if the Standard Conditions of Sale are used. SCS 3.1.2 (e) provides the property is sold subject to 'public requirements' which include (SCS 1.1.1 (j)) 'any notice, order or proposal given or made (whether before or after the date of the contract) by a body acting on statutory authority'. By s. 6(1) of the 1994 Act, the s. 3 covenant for title will not be breached in respect of any matter subject to which the property is in fact sold as a result of this condition.

The report of the Parliamentary special committee (HL Paper 62 Session 1993–4) does not throw a glaringly clear light on the important issue of whether a wide or narrow view will be given to the concept of 'third-party rights'. Overall I would suggest the view from the tenor of the report that what is intended is 'proprietary rights' (see p. 3) in the traditional sense. But against this, of course, is the obvious emphasis given to the view that the covenants have been 'modernised and expressed in plain English' (see p. 5). A very useful distinction was made in the previous law. General powers and obligations under legislation such as the town and country planning legislation did not have to be disclosed to prospective purchasers (see, e.g., *Coles* v *White City (Manchester) Greyhound Association Ltd* (1929) 45 TLR 230).

Such matters in any event come within s. 3(2). But where the statutory powers give rise to rights exercisable against particular property there could be a defect of title (see, e.g., *Re Leyland and Taylor's Contract* [1900] 2 Ch 625 concerning a notice to pave). The same distinction could be drawn in deciding which of these statutory rights are rights exercisable by third parties within the implied covenant.

Freedom from encumbrances — limited title guarantee

If only a limited title guarantee is given the covenant for freedom from encumbrances is found in s. 3(3) of the 1994 Act. The effect is to limit the covenant to encumbrances coming into being since the last disposition for value. The definition of the matters which are within s. 3(3) is the same generally as for s. 3(1). The exception in s. 3(2) for certain rights conferred by enactments does not apply, however, because it is irrelevant as s. 3(3) applies only to rights made, granted or suffered to be made by the covenantor.

The last disposition for value

The s. 3(3) covenant applies only to things done since the last disposition for value.

'Disposition' is defined in s. 1(4) to include the creation of a term of years. 'Value' is not defined in the Act. This is, however, a term of art in property law and here must be given its usual technical meaning. Value in this sense means money or money's worth. This includes any non-monetary consideration of actual value (see, e.g., *Thorndike v Hunt* (1859) 3 De G & J 563). Value includes marriage where the disposition is made in view of a future marriage (*Attorney-General v Jacobs Smith* [1895] 2 QB 341). It does not include a disposition made in respect of a past marriage.

The last disposition for value is not necesarily the disposition under which the covenantor purchased and investigated the prior title. For example, where a personal representative, beneficiary or trustee is selling it may be some time since the last disposition for value and in the interval things may have happened of which the seller is unaware.

Scope of the covenant

The covenant under s. 3(3) is limited compared to the covenant under s. 3(1) by the way it is expressed. The s. 3(3) covenant refers to three matters:

(a) that, at the time of making the disposition, no charges, encumbrances or third-party rights subsist that have been created by the covenantor since the last disposition for value;

(b) that, at the time of making the disposition, no charges, encumbrances or third-party rights subsist that the covenantor has suffered to be created since the last disposition for value;

(c) that the covenantor is not aware that, since the last disposition for value, anyone else has created or suffered to be created any charges, encumbrances or third-party rights which subsist at the time of making the disposition.

So far as (a), (b) and (c) are concerned the definitions of charges, encumbrances and rights must follow s. 3(1). Precisely the same words clearly describe the same categories of interests.

A new concept is introduced of 'suffering' the property to be charged or encumbered or subjected to third-party rights. This will cover cases where encumbrances and charges and third-party rights can come into being without the act of the covenantor. Rights arising by adverse possession are one possible example, such as the easement in *E. R. Ives Investment Ltd* v *Hugh* [1967] 2 QB 739. Another possible application is where the covenantor (say a trustee or tenant for life) has acquiesced in the creation of an encumbrance by a previous estate owner at a time after the last conveyance for value.

The last part of this covenant is the covenant that the covenantor is not 'aware' that anyone else has created rights or suffered them to be created. In *Sindall plc* v *Cambridgeshire CC* [1994] 3 All ER 932 CA the court, though 'not aware', implied a representation by a seller that reasonable enquiries had been made. But that was in the context of replies to preiminary enquiries.

In plain English 'aware' must indicate a subjective state of actual awareness and has no connotation of an objective state of 'ought to be aware'. This creates a difficulty if the agent of the covenantor has the requisite awareness but the covenantor does not. For example, a firm of solicitors may act over a period of time for a large estate. The present seller — say the tenant for life — may be quite unaware of some encumbrance created in the past. Is the knowledge of the solicitor to be imparted to the covenantor for the purposes of s. 3(3)? On principle the answer is indubitably to be yes. The solicitor is an agent and the general principle of agency is *qui facit per alium facit per se*. More precisely any knowledge received by an agent in the course of the agent's authority and which the agent has a duty to pass on to the principal is deemed to be the knowledge of the principal (see, e.g., *Tanham* v *Nicholson* (1872) LR 5 HL 561; *Wyllie* v *Pollen* (1863) 32 LJ Ch 782). If a solicitor acting in a conveyancing matter does have knowledge of an encumbrance affecting the property then he or she most clearly has a duty to inform the client of its existence.

Caution in practice

The client will in practice not be aware of the nature of the obligations under s. 3 of the 1994 Act. It is, therefore, advisable for the seller's solicitor to ensure that the seller is made aware of the need to disclose and deal in the contract with any encumbrance affecting the property which could fall within the covenant for title. This will be dealt with as a matter of routine practice when taking instructions from the client.

Covenants relating to leasehold land

Grant of a lease

Where the disposition is the grant of a lease then the covenants discussed above can be imposed by use of the same introductory words as on a freehold sale — that is, 'with full title guarantee' of 'with limited title guarantee'. The previous system of covenants for title did not apply on the grant of a lease (Law of Property Act 1925, s. 76(5)) and this is on the face of it a significant change.

It is most unlikely that the necessary words to imply a covenant for title will be used where there is a grant of a lease at a rack rent with no premium. The possibility of using the new covenants is greater where there is a grant of a long lease at a premium. This has always been viewed as more akin to a freehold sale requiring from the sensible purchaser an investigation of the freehold title.

The effect of giving the covenant for title in the grant of a lease is:

(a)   There is a covenant that the landlord has the right to grant the lease (s. 2(1)) and will make good that promise in the Land Registry (s. 2(2)). The latter part of the obligation is not entirely clear from the wording of the Act. Section 2(2)(b) requires the covenantor to establish to the satisfaction of the Chief Land Registrar the right of the lessee to be registered as proprietor. There are, of course, two main classes of leasehold title. These are leasehold title absolute and good leasehold title. For the former to be granted by the Land Registry then either the freehold and other reversionary title has to be already registered or at the time of registration it has to be proved to the satisfaction of the Chief Land Registrar.

If the Standard conditions of Sale (3rd ed.) are used in the transaction then SCS 8.2.4 will be important. This states that where the term of the lease will exceed 21 years, the seller is to deduce a title which will enable the buyer to register the lease at the Land Registry with an absolute title. If SCS 8.2.4 is not omitted it is clear what title the seller purports to grant and, thus, what is the scope in this regard of the covenant for title. If SCS 8.2.4 is removed it should for certainty be made clear in the contract that the covenant for title extends only to obtaining good leasehold title (see appendix 1, No. 20) if that is what the seller intends.

(b)   There is a covenant that the title is free from encumbrances in the way described already above. It is perfectly clear that s. 3(1) or s. 3(3) cannot be satisfied in most cases where there are encumbrances on the freehold or other reversionary title. There are differences in this respect because of the more narrow form of the covenant for freedom from encumbrances given under s. 3(3) where there is only limited title guarantee. However, the basic point is the same — there may be encumbrances on the freehold or reversionary title which will lead to a covenantor granting a lease being in breach of the s. 3 covenant for title.

Suppose, for example, that there is a restrictive covenant binding the freehold estate. If the full title guarantee is given then breach of the covenant for title given by the lessor is very likely. If the lease is granted with limited title guarantee then the freeholder may very well not be in breach of the covenant for title because the restrictive covenant may have been created before the last disposition for value.

Further leasehold covenant (s. 4)

If a disposition is of leasehold land and is expressed to be made with full title guarantee or with limited title guarantee then there is implied the covenant in s. 4 of the 1994 Act. This covenant is to the effect that the lease is outstanding at the time of the disposition and there is no subsisting breach of a term of the lease or anything which would render the lease liable to forfeiture. This covenant is applied in the same way to the same effect to an underlease (s. 4(2)) and presumably any sub-underlease or further derivative lease.

The s. 4 covenant replaces the covenant applied in unregistered land by the Law of Property Act 1925, s. 76(1)(a). This is a covenant which will commonly be amended in practice. Usually on the sale of a very long lease the seller is unwilling to guarantee that there is no existing breach of a repairing covenant. The fact has long been recognised by the Standard Conditions of Sale in use in conveyancing. The current edition provides a widely accepted variation of the former covenant of title (see SCS 8.1.4 (2nd ed.); 3.2.1 or 3.2.3 (3rd ed. — in force from 1 July 1995)). For suggested amendments see appendix 1, Nos. 16 and 17).

Further covenant where there is a mortgage of leasehold land or land subject to a rentcharge (s. 5)

The further covenants in s. 5 apply to a mortgage of property if it is subject to a rentcharge and also to a mortgage of leasehold land. 'Mortgage' here includes charge (s. 5(4)). The covenant under s. 5

reflects the covenants given formerly under s. 76 of the Law of Property Act 1925 and are not problematic. They apply whether the disposition is made with full title guarantee or with limited title guarantee. The effect is as follows:

(a)   On a mortgage of land, either with full or limited title guarantee, there is implied the following covenant if the land is subject to a *rentcharge*. This is a covenant that the mortgagor will *fully and promptly* observe and perform the obligations in the instrument creating the rentcharge *which are enforceable with respect to the property by the owner of the rentcharge in the owner's capacity as such* (s. 5(2)).

(b)   On a mortgage of leasehold land there is implied a covenant that the mortgagor will *fully and promptly* observe and perform the obligations which the lease imposes upon the mortgagor in the capacity of tenant.

In a mortgage the mortgagor will invariably in practice be required to give a full title guarantee. This is because the lender is in a position to stipulate the form of covenant to be given.

Limited effect of covenants (s. 6)

The covenants given by a seller obviously cannot be absolute in their effect. Important limitations on the effect of the covenants are contained in s. 6 of the Act.

Making the disposition expressly subject to encumbrances

First of all the disposition may be made subject to any defect in the title, or any charge, encumbrance or third-party right to which the disposition is expressly made subject.

So far as the seller is concerned this requires careful steps to be taken. The seller's solicitor should identify any matters which the sale is to be made subject to. Full disclosure of these matters must then be made to the buyer. This is best done in the contract by a formal condition setting out the relevant matters and stating that the sale is made subject to them and accordingly that those matters cannot be made the subject of requisitions or objections on title. Full and frank disclosure of such a matter is essential if the seller is to be able to enforce the contract and make the purchaser buy subject to an encumbrance or defect of which the seller is aware.

These encumbrances need to be mentioned in the contract but not necessarily set out in the subsequent transfer (see SCS 3rd ed., 4.5.3 which was introduced to make this proposition clear).

Things within the knowledge of the buyer

Section 6(2) in any event provides that the covenants do not apply to anything which at the time of the disposition is within the actual knowledge of the covenantee (s. 6(2)(a)). To this is added a provision that the covenant does not apply to anything 'which is a necessary consequence of facts that are then within the actual knowledge' of the covenantee. The first part of this rule is fairly clear. The actual knowledge of the covenantee is best established in practice by setting out the relevant matters in the contract or other disposition. The second part of this rule refers to anything which is 'a necessary consequence of facts' which are within the covenantee's knowledge. This is by no means so clear in its effect. What kind of encumbrance, charge, right or defect in title is a necessary consequence of a known fact?

An example which suggests itself is as follows. The buyer knows the seller has not paid the entire purchase price. It is a necessary consequence of this fact that the property *may* be subject to an unpaid seller's lien. It is not, however, a necessary consequence that it actually *is* subject to an unpaid sellers' lien. In a variety of circumstances the lien may not exist or be effective!

A further example shows the difficulty of bringing any case precisely within these words. The buyer may know there is a track over the land. The existence of a right of way which is an encumbrance is a possible not a necessary consequence of this fact. It may well be that s. 6(2) will be held to mean that the purchase is subject to the track (of which the purchaser has knowledge) whatever its legal status. All that is certain is that the subsection is uncertain in its scope.

The relationship between this provision and the warranty of title given in SCS 3 is discussed below (page 34 *et seq*). The position of 'patent' defects of title is also discussed there.

For the purpose of s. 6 of the 1994 Act, the Law of Property Act 1925, s. 198, does not apply (see s. 6(3)). Section 198 provides that registration is deemed to be notice of the thing registered. The precise words are:

> The registration of any instrument or matter in any register kept under the Land Charges Act 1972 or any local land charges register shall be deemed to constitute actual notice of such instrument or matter, and of the fact of such registration, to all persons and for all purposes concerned with the land affected, as from the date of registration or other prescribed date and so long as the registration continues in force.

The effect of the disregard of this important provision by s. 6(3) of the 1994 Act requires careful explanation. Suppose A is the owner of Blackacre and B has the benefit of a restrictive covenant over Blackacre. This covenant should, in the case of unregistered land, be registered in the Land Charges Register as a class D(ii) land charge. Assuming A, on a sale to C, gives a covenant for title and the existence of the land charge is a breach of this then the effect of s. 6(3) is that A cannot insist that C knew of the restrictive covenant because of its registration in the Land Charges Register. A may, despite the fact that C should have carried out a simple search and discovered this restriction, be liable for breach of the implied covenant for title. C, of course, is most likely still to be bound by the restrictive covenant and that is the substance of C's complaint against A.

Passing the benefit of covenants (s. 7)

Section 7 of the 1994 Act provides that the benefit of a covenant implied by virtue of the Act belongs to the estate or interest of the covenantee and can be enforced by any person in whom that estate or interest is vested in whole or in part for the time being.

The essential effect of the section is straightforward. Once a purchaser has the benefit of a covenant then any subsequent purchaser also has the benefit. Where a disposition is made with full title guarantee or in some cases with limited title guarantee this can lead in theory to a number of persons being liable for the same defect.

Suppose a builder sells a house to a buyer and gives the full title guarantee. There will be a breach of the covenant if, for example, the builder has already sold a strip of the garden to another purchaser. The buyer of the house may resell to C and C to D and D to E. On a housing estate such a sequence of sales can happen very quickly (in the right economic conditions). E may discover during a quarrel with a neighbour that the strip of land in question had in fact left the ownership of the builder before B purchased. E will be able to sue the builder and C and D for breach of the covenant for title.

The literal construction of s. 7 is not consonant with its clear purpose. The benefit of the covenant for title is said to be enforceable 'by every person in whom that estate or interest is (in whole or in part) for the time being vested'. This is presumably meant to apply where the land to which the benefit is attached is physically divided. However, an estate in land may be divided in terms of interest — into a life interest and a remainder; into a lease, a sublease and a sub-underlease and so on. Taking the words of this section literally, each part of the estate in interest would be able to enforce the covenant. This wording is very slightly changed from the equivalent provision in the Law of Property Act 1925, s. 76(6) (the words 'for the whole or any part thereof' are changed to 'in whole or in part'). The change is clearly not intended to alter the effect of the provision. Thus, the benefit runs with parts of the land when it is physically divided but not when it is divided in interest.

One problem which both the old and the new provision do not assist with is this. The purchaser may, under the transfer or conveyance in question, receive no interest at all in the land purported to be conveyed. In this case the purchaser may sue the seller on the implied covenant for title but cannot sue any predecessor. The predecessor's covenant attaches to the land and runs with it but the present purchaser owns no land to which that covenant has attached. See *Onward Building Society* v *Smithson*

[1893] 1 Ch 1 in which a rogue who had purchased land from D obtained by a trick a second conveyance from D and then mortgaged the land using that title to P. Lindley LJ said (at p. 12), 'Now, apart from the question of estoppel, the plaintiffs, as assignees of a mere equity of redemption, have no remedy against the defendants on their covenants for title, for there is no legal estate with which the covenants could run'.

Welsh form of covenant (s. 8(4))

Instead of 'with full title guarantee' the expression 'gyda gwarant teitl llawn' may be used. Instead of 'with limited title guarantee' the expression 'gyda gwarant teitl cyfyngedig' may be used. Either of these expressions may be used whether or not the rest of the document is in Welsh, whether or not the document is made in Wales and whether or not the land concerned or any of it is in Wales. The drafter of this Act evidently quailed at the prospect of rendering in Welsh the actual content of the covenants, and the content of the covenant is thus, regrettably, given only in the English version.

Construction of covenants (s. 8(2))

Section 8(2) provides that ss. 81 and 83 of the Law of Property Act 1925 apply to covenants implied under the 1994 Act. These two sections as follows:

81.   Effect of covenant with two or more jointly
(1)   A covenant, and a contract under seal, and a bond or obligation under seal, made with two or more jointly, to pay money or to make a conveyance, or to do any other act, to them or for their benefit, shall be deemed to include, and shall, by virtue of this Act, imply, an obligation to do the act to, or for the benefit of, the survivor or survivors of them, and to, or for the benefit of, any other person to whom the right to sue on the covenant, contract, bond, or obligation devolves, and where made after the commencement of this Act shall be construed as being also made with each of them.
(2)   This section extends to a covenant implied by virtue of this Act.

(3) This section applies only if and as far as a contrary intention is not expressed in the covenant, contract, bond, or obligation, and has effect subject to the covenant, contract, bond, or obligation, and to the provisions therein contained.

(4) Except as otherwise expressly provided, this section applies to a covenant, contract, bond, or obligation made or implied after the 31st day of December, 1881.

(5) In its application to instruments made after the coming into force of section 1 of the Law of Property (Miscellaneous Provisions) Act 1989 [which come into force on 31 July 1990] subsection (1) above shall have effect as if for the words 'under seal, and a bond or obligation under seal,' there were substituted the words 'bond or obligation executed as a deed in accordance with section 1 of the Law of Property (Miscellaneous Provisions) Act 1989'.

The effect of this wordy provision is that if there is more than one covenantee then each can enforce the covenant separately. The implication can be negated by the instrument creating the disposition (s. 81(3)) but it is difficult to imagine any circumstances where it would be necessary to do so.

83. Construction of implied covenants

In the construction of a covenant or proviso, or other provision, implied in a deed or assent by virtue of this Act, words importing the singular or plural number, or the masculine gender, shall be read as also importing the plural or singular number, or as extending to females, as the case may require.

The purpose of this is perfectly clear. Words importing the female gender are not required by this wording to be read as importing the male gender. In fact the covenants set out in the Act itself are all written using the single masculine gender. Presumably, this rule of construction will apply to variations of the implied covenant in particular dispositions and some thought must be given to how these are expressed. As to express words in the conveyance s. 61, LPA 1925 should also be considered.

Transitional provisions

Covenants given before 1 July 1995 (s. 10)

The 1994 Act has no effect on dispositions made before it came into force. In theory covenants in old form may continue to have currency for a considerable time in the future. As is the case with the new covenants the benefit passes with the benefited land. A purchaser may, thus, have the benefit of both the former covenant against a previous owner and the new form of covenant against a later seller. The old forms of covenants are set out for ease of comparison in appendix 3.

Overlapping cases (s. 11)

Section 11 provides for the giving of covenants in the old form (see appendix 3) in certain cases after the commencement of the 1994 Act. The conditions to be satisfied for this to be so are:

(a)   The disposition must be made 'in pursuance of a contract' entered into before 1 July 1995 (s. 11(1) and (2)).

(b)   For the covenants in the Law of Property Act 1925, s. 76, to be implied, the contract must contain a requirement for the disposition to be made with the old form of covenant for title (s. 11(1)).

(c)   For the covenant in the Land Registration Act 1925, s. 24(1)(a), to be implied on a disposition of a leasehold interest the disposition must be one to which that paragraph would have applied if it had been made before 1 July 1995.

(d)   The instrument effecting the disposition must refer to the contract pursuant to which it is made (s. 11(1)(b) and (2)(b)).

(e)   The old covenants will not be applied if there has been what is called an 'intervening disposition' with full title guarantee. An intervening disposition is one made on or after 1 July 1995 to the person by whom the disposition in question is made or a predecessor in title of that person (s. 11(3)). In the case of the covenants implied under the Law of Property Act 1925, s. 76, the covenants are not implied if there is an 'intervening disposition' made with full title guarantee. In the case of the covenant implied under the Land Registration Act 1925, s. 24(1)(a), the covenant is not implied if there has been an intervening disposition of the leasehold interest made with full title guarantee.

The expression 'contract' is not defined in the act and it does pose one very clear problem. The most obvious case when the transitional provision will apply is when the disposition is made subject to an option entered into before 1 July 1995. The juridical nature of an option was much discussed following the failure of the Law of Property (Miscellaneous Provisions) Act 1989, s. 2, to deal properly with the position of options. The issue, the relevant authorities and opinions were all dealt with by Hoffmann J in *Spiro* v *Glencrown Properties Ltd* [1991] Ch 537. His lordship gave the following view:

> An option is not strictly speaking either an offer or a conditional contract. It does not have *all* the incidents of the standard form of either of these concepts. To that extent it is a relationship *sui generis*. But there are ways in which it resembles each of them.

An option may be found in many forms of contract. It may be found in what is described as an option contract or option agreement; it may be found in a variety of leasehold instruments; it may be found as a part of a conveyance or transfer. There can be no doubt at all that a future court will take the same clearly sensible approach as in *Spiro* v *Glencrown Properties Ltd*. The option is the legal agreement by which the parties determine their future rights including the covenants for title in the event of a disposition pursuant to the option. The court will construe a disposition made pursuant to an option as a disposition made pursuant to a contract within s. 11 of the 1994 Act and will do that in whatever form of document the option is found. This is probably the intended but not the wholly clear effect of s. 13 of the Act. This provides that where there is a disposition in accordance with an option, 'the contract for the disposition shall be deemed to have been entered into on the grant of the option'. This does not quite say, as it should, that all options will be deemed to be contracts within s. 11 of the Act but it may be presumed to have the intended and desired effect. For the purpose of the transitional provisions the exercise of an option granted before 1 July 1995 the commencement of this Part will be treated as a disposition in pursuance of a contract entered into before commencement.

Cases where there is an 'intervening disposition' (s. 12)

The 'overlapping case' provisions do not apply where there has been an intervening disposition as discussed above. Instead s. 12 applies. An example will illustrate how this works.

A contracts to sell Blackacre to B. B contracts to sell Blackacre to C. B's contract with C is made before 1 July 1995 and provides for B to convey as beneficial owner. It makes no difference necessarily to the outcome whether A's contract is made before 1 July 1995. The important fact is that on or after 1 July 1995 A does dispose of the property to B and gives full title guarantee. Now there is an intervening disposition and the covenant C obtains will be governed by s. 12. The covenants to be given to C by B will be as follows:

(a) If B has contracted to convey as beneficial owner then B will convey with full title guarantee (s. 12(2)).

(b) If B has contracted to convey as settlor, trustee, mortgagee or personal representative then B will convey with limited title guarantee (s. 12(3)).

(c) For the purposes of s. 12 there is a particular rule of construction in respect of a contract for the disposition of a leasehold interest which is already registered. This is to be 'construed as requiring the person making the disposition for which it provides to do so by an instrument expressed to be made with full title guarantee' (s. 12(4)). Presumably this rule of construction is not mandatory. Section 12(4) suggests the rule is mandatory, but surely this (construction) will not be applied if the contract expressly negates the imposition of such or any covenant for title.

(d) Some difficulty of construction may arise when the contract has provided for a particular variation of the covenant implied by the Law of Property Act 1925, s. 76, or the Land Registration Act 1925, s. 24(1)(a). In such a case s. 12(5) of the 1994 Act provides that the covenant implied under the 1994 Act is to be implied 'with a corresponding modification'.

3

Practical Use of the Covenants for Title

The position where no covenant for title is given

The robust stance taken by a conservative lawyer faced with the Law of Property (Miscellaneous Provisions) Act 1994 will be to refuse to give any covenant of title at all and be done with the matter. It is unlikely, given the influence of institutional lenders on the conveyancing market, that this stance can be maintained. The question of whether it is a realistic one will be approached by posing a slightly different question, namely, whether there is any reason why a seller should be unwilling to give the full title guarantee.

It should be noted that the Standard Conditions of Sale (3rd ed. SCS, 4.5.2) provide for 'full title guarantee' as the default position. If no or a lesser covenant is given this must be varied by a special condition e.g., by inserting 'No Title Guarantee is Given' in the relevant front page space.

Should a seller be unwilling to give a full title guarantee?

In practice there is no compulsion for a seller to give any covenants for title at all except in the cases where particular covenants for title are stipulated by statute. For the rest the covenant to be given is a matter of bargaining between the buyer and the seller. In conveyancing practice this has in general been the subject of little dispute or concern, the pattern of circumstances in which the different covenants are given being well known and understood in the profession. The 1994 Act changes this happy consensus. Persons drafting contracts for sale now have to decide what covenants for title to offer and persons accepting or rejecting the proferred terms must decide what covenants for title to accept. In the special circumstances of commercial conveyancing it can be expected that this will be frequently a highly contentious matter — though solicitors as ever will presumably resist the temptation to wrangle needlessly at the expense of their clients.

The relevance of the Standard Conditions of Sale

It is important in analysing the effect of the new covenants for title not to lose sight of the effect of the contractual terms set out in the conditions of sale. A number of these are very relevant when considering the practical significance of arguments over the effect of the covenants for title.

SCS 3

This contains a fairly extensive promise by the seller to sell the property free from encumbrances. The exceptions to this promise are set out in SCS 3.1.2 as follows:

The incumbrances subject to which the property is sold are:
(a)   those mentioned in the agreement
(b)   those discoverable by inspection of the property before the contract
(c)   those the seller does not and could not know about
(d)   entries made before the date of the contract in any public register except those maintained by HM Land Registry or its Land Charges Department or by Companies House
(e)   public requirements.

The promise in SCS 3 to sell the property free from encumbrances covers very much the same ground as the covenant given by s. 3 of the 1994 Act.

SCS 7.4

This provides that 'completion does not cancel liability to perform any outstanding obligation under the contract'. In considering the importance of the implied covenants for title this is a very important link in the chain of analysis. The doctrine of merger is a general principle of English law. It provides that where a contract is to be implemented by a further instrument then once that instrument is executed the rights and remedies of the parties derive from that instrument and not from the contract. Thus, in routine conveyancing the rights of the parties under the contract are said to merge in the conveyance or transfer and then depend largely upon the covenants for title given in that instrument. The effect of SCS 7.4 is to negate the operation of the doctrine of merger altogether. This means that even if no covenant for title is given the buyer can sue on the warranty given by SCS 3 if it has in fact been given.

SCS 8.1.4

The significance of this provision in dealing with leasehold property has already been discussed above (page 23).

SCS 8.2.4

This provides that on the grant of a lease:

> If the term of the new lease will exceed 21 years, the seller is to deduce a title which will enable the buyer to register the lease at HM Land Registry with an absolute title.

This provision clearly renders irrelevant much of the ground covered by the covenant for title under s. 2 of the Act.

Summary

Table 3.1 gives a summary of how the position varies depending whether the SCS warranty of title is included. Column 1 states a particular defect in title. Column 2 briefly summarises the application of the full title guarantee, column 3 the limited title guarantee. Columns 4 and 5 summarise the position if there is no covenant for title but the SCS have been used: in column 4 with the doctrine of merger not applying and in column 5 with the doctrine of merger applying (SCS 7.4 removed).

Defect	Full title guarantee	Limited title guarantee	SCS unamended	SCS with SCS 7.4 removed
The seller has no title to the land at all.	Breach of s. 2(1)(a).	Breach of s. 2(1)(a).	No remedy in the absence of express warranty as to title, fraud, misrepresentation, undue influence or other vitiating factor.	
The Land Registry refuses registration because of a technical defect.	Breach of and liability under s. 2(1)(b) to meet requisitions at seller's expense.	Breach of s. 2(1)(b) to meet requisitions at seller's expense.	No remedy in the absence of the above factors.	
The property is subject to an undisclosed right of way.	Seller liable under s. 3(1) unless the seller could not reasonably be expected to know or the buyer knew of the defect (s. 6).	Seller liable under s. 3(3) if the seller created the encumbrance or allowed it to be created.	Seller liable for breach of SCS 3 but not if it is a patent defect.	Seller not liable after completion in the absence of express warranty as to title, fraud, misrepresentation, undue influence or other vitiating factor.

37

Patent defects in title

It may be helpful to summarise how the SCS and the new covenants for title apply to patent defects of title. At common law a patent defect is one which the purchaser should discover by the usual inspections of the property (see *Yandle & Sons* v *Sutton* [1922] Ch 199). Suppose in a particular case a reasonable purchaser should discover that there is a pipeline across the property and this constitutes a matter of title. There may be a breach of the covenant for title if this defect comes within the covenant. We may assume that the right to use the pipeline may be a right exercisable by a third party. If there is nothing in the contract of relevance to this matter (i.e., SCS 3 — warranty and disclosure — is omitted), the purchaser may have an action on the covenant for title notwithstanding the fact that the defect in question was a patent defect. This is so even if the defect is apparent on the face of the conveyance (see *Page* v *Midland Railway Co.* [1894] 1 Ch 11). However, the standard conditions of sale (SCS 3.1.2 (b)) provide that the property is sold subject to matters which are 'discoverable by inspection of the property before the contract'. The purchaser will not be able to enforce the covenant for title so far as the breach comes within this provision. Section 6(2) of the 1994 Act provides that the covenant does not cover anything within the actual knowledge of the covenantee. This is a narrower range of things than those which fall within SCS 3.1.2 (b) and, thus, where SCS 3.1.2 (b) is included in the contract, the effect of the statutory covenant is in fact less than the warranty given by the conditions for sale.

Relevance of other remedies

Even where the doctrine of merger does apply to a conveyance (where the Standard Conditions of Sale are used in cases where SCS 7.4 is excluded) then there are still remedies available to the purchaser after completion other than the covenants for title:

(a)   It is a clear principle that a contract can be rescinded for mistake even though it has been executed (*Solle* v *Butcher* [1950] 1 KB 671). Rescission for mistake has to be looked at in the light of SCS 7.1.3 which permits rescission only in the case of fraud or recklessness or where the property is substantially different from the contractual description.

(b) It has for some time been the rule that a contract can be rescinded for misrepresentation even though it has been executed. *Seddon* v *North Eastern Salt Co. Ltd* [1905] 1 Ch 326 provided a rule to the contrary but this was abrogated by the Misrepresentation Act 1967, s. 1(b). Thus, if a statement as to title involves a misrepresentation of fact then rescission may be available even after completion. Also damages may be available under s. 2(1) of the Misrepresentation Act 1967 where the conditions of that section are satisfied. Again the remedies available may be affected by SCS 7.

(c) In appropriate cases the purchaser may have a remedy for fraud or undue influence. This is a possibility only faintly connected to the matter in hand and, consequently, is not discussed further.

Summary of the no-convenant position

A seller who refuses to give a covenant for title will wish to amend the Standard Conditions of Sale. This will be done by removing or limiting the warranty for title in SCS 3 and by removing the declaration of non-merger in SCS 7.4. The effect of SCS 4.5.2 (3rd ed.) will also be regarded by an express statement that no title guarantee is given. There will, however, still remain liability for remedies that arise outside the contract such as for misrepresentation.

The position of mortgagees

To those involved in conveyancing practice it would seem that the position of mortgagees would become an important determinant of what pattern of covenants for title would be expected in the future.

Covenants in the mortgage

It goes almost without the need for comment that the mortgagor will in the mortgage covenant with full title guarantee. The lender is in a position to stipulate the covenants that are to be provided and will demand the full guarantee. In practice the covenant by the mortgagor is, however, of virtually no value. The mortgagee is interested in the land as such only when the mortgagor defaults on the loan and the mortgagor is rarely, thereafter, in a position to be worth suing on the covenant.

Benefit of previous covenants

Should the mortgagee insist that the transfer or other assurance to the mortgagor is given with particular covenants for title — the preferred obviously being the full title guarantee? Under s. 7 of the 1994 Act the benefit of the covenant for title runs with the land. If A purchases land from B and mortgages that land to C and the transfer from B to A is with full or limited title guarantee then, by s. 7, the benefit of the statutory covenants 'shall be annexed and incident to, and shall go with, the estate or interest of the person to whom the disposition is made'. Under the previous law a mortgagee did not acquire the benefit of the covenant given to the mortgagor. This was because, although the covenant ran with the land the mortgagee did not have the same estate in the land. The position is almost certainly the same under s. 7. The mortgagee cannot enforce the covenant given to the mortgagor or the mortgagor's predecessor in title. In the discussion above of s. 7 (page 26) it was noted that there is a possible ambiguity which would allow the mortgagee to have the benefit of those covenants, but that cannot be the intended purpose of s. 7, as is explained in that discussion. This analysis can be taken a stage further. The mortgagee may sell as mortgagee in possession and in that case has the benefit of the Law of Property Act 1925, s. 104. This section states that:

(1)   A mortgagee exercising the power of sale conferred by this Act shall have power, by deed, to convey the property sold, for such estate and interest therein as he is by this Act authorised to sell or convey or may be the subject of the mortgage.

The purchaser from the mortgagee will, thus, obtain the same estate as the mortgagor had and will have the benefit of the covenant for title given to the mortgagor and the mortgagor's predecessors in title.

It is worth returning to the example already introduced. A purchases land from B and mortgages this land to C. C takes possession as mortgagee and sells to D. Suppose that unknown to the parties at the time of each transaction the land was the subject of a long-forgotten easement of way which a troublesome neighbour is now seeking to enforce. B has given A a covenant with full title guarantee and may well be in breach of his covenant (see discussion above). A gave C a full title guarantee and again may be in breach of this but is now insolvent. D will have the benefit of B's covenant but not the covenant which A has given to C. The covenant given to a mortgagee cannot pass to a purchaser from the mortgagee as that is a purchase of a different estate or interest from that held by the mortgagee. D will have, therefore, the benefit of B's covenant and any covenant given to D by C.

It should be mentioned to complete this picture that mortgagees paid little attention to covenants for title given under the 'old regime'. The main safeguard for the mortgagee in respect of the security offered is the investigation of title by the mortgagee's solicitor. Since the solicitor's report on title is obliged to confirm that the title offered is an acceptable title (within the terms of the instructions from the lender), the covenant for title given by the seller to the mortgagor makes little commercial difference to the eventual value of the security.

Covenants for title in registered land

The relevant provisions of the Land Registration Act 1925 and the Land Registration Rules 1925 are reproduced for convenience in appendix 4 and appendix 5. The new rules for covenants for title are in the Land Registration (Implied Covenants for Title) Rules 1995 which are reproduced in appendix 6. Under the pre-1995 regime the precise effect of the covenants for title in registered land has been the subject of prolonged and largely fruitless controversy (see *Emmet on Title*, 19th ed., release 3, 14.013, where the arguments are reviewed and further references given). A great deal of the controversy lay in the curiously unhelpful wording of the Land Registration Rules 1925, r. 77. This led some to take the view that because a registered land title is subject to overriding interests in any event, the covenant for title can give a purchaser little assistance because, in any event, what is transferred by the seller is what the seller actually owns. The covenant for title operates only if the transfer fails to transfer what the seller has promised to convey and is accordingly largely meaningless.

What is the position under the new statutory covenants for title as far as registered land is concerned? As was previously the case, covenants for title will not be entered on the register of title (see Land Registration Rules 1925, rr. 76 and 76A). It is considered that this will cause some problem in suing a previous covenantee because it will never be apparent from the register of title what covenant a previous transferor gave. Indeed it will not even be apparent in most cases what previous transferees there have been. Previous transfers of the land may be available from the Land Registry (see Land Registry Practice Leaflet No. 19).

Particular effect of covenants in registered land

The covenant under s. 2(1)(a), 'the right to dispose', is clearly relevant to registered land cases. In many instances the transferor may not purport to be the registered proprietor but claim the right to convey as personal representative or whatever. Circumstances can readily be envisaged where this claim turns out to be unfounded. Unlike the pre-1995 covenant this applies where the seller has no title, or has never any title to the land (see above page 9).

The covenant for freedom from encumbrances under s. 3 of the 1994 Act poses more difficulty. Rule 77A of the Land Registration Rules 1925 provides that the covenant takes effect as if it is subject to all entries on the register *at the time of the execution* of the disposition. It is possible to conceive of cases where entries on the register are made after the execution of the disposition. Normally this will not occur in a case of a sale or mortgage because the purchaser or mortgagee will have the benefit of a Land Registry search giving priority over any subsequent dealing with the registered land. This, though, may not always be the case. The covenant could thus conceivably be broken by a later registration.

Rule 77A provides also that the disposition is subject to any overriding interest of which the purchaser has notice. This is different from the requirement of s. 6(2) that the covenant does not extend to anything within the actual knowledge of the covenantee or which is a necessary consequence of facts that are within the covenantee's actual knowledge. The concept of notice in r. 77A seems to exclude a wider range of matters from the operation of the covenant. A person may have 'notice' — constructive notice — of any matter which would be discovered by making the investigations which should reasonably be made in the circumstances. But s. 6(2) limits constructive notice to something 'which is a necessary consequence of facts that are then within the actual knowledge' of the covenantee. It is not clear whether 'imputed notice' (that is, notice which the covenantee's solicitor has) falls within s. 6(2). This is discussed further above (page 25). In contrast imputed notice clearly falls within the term 'notice' in r. 77A so as to exclude overriding interests of which the covenantee has imputed notice.

The area which remains controversial is the case of overriding interests of which the purchaser has no notice. In respect of these there will be no breach of the covenant given by s. 2 because the title which the covenantor purports to convey is a registered title. In respect of these overriding interests there may be breach of the covenant given by s. 3 — freedom from encumbrances. Such an overriding interest can fall within the wording of s. 3 without doubt. The argument mounted in respect of the pre-1995 law to suggest that these overriding interests are not within the covenant would run as follows if applied to the 1994 Act. Section 3 is a covenant that 'the property' is free from encumbrances in the manner defined by s. 3. The property in question is registered land, that is, a specified title subject to the registered matters and overriding interests which affect it. This circular piece of reasoning leaves no scope for the operation of the implied covenant. If a court gave effect to this view it would be accepting that Parliament and the Law Commission were content to engage in a substantially worthless exercise so far as defining the scope of the implied covenants is concerned. There can be no doubt that should the question arise the court will hold that the new covenant for title does apply to overriding interests of which the purchaser has no notice. It may do this by holding that the 'property' in s. 3 is given the meaning of the land rather than 'the registered title in question'. Section 3 and r. 77A together, then, make the position clear. The covenant does not extend to matters on the register or to overriding interests of which the transferee has notice but otherwise it is effective.

It is worth following one example through. The land in question is a large estate. Lord South, the estate owner, grants a 20-year lease to Mr West. This task is handled by Lord South's estate office. Fifteen years later a parcel of the estate (which is registered land) is transferred to Mr East. After the transfer it turns out that Mr West's lease includes some of this parcel. The lease to Mr West is an overriding interest under the Land Registration Act 1925, s. 70(1)(b). It is an encumbrance which falls within s. 3 of the 1994 Act and is not excluded as a matter which the seller 'could not reasonably be expected to know about'. If the Standard Conditions of Sale were used then there is a warranty (SCS 3.1.1) that the seller is selling free from encumbrances except as mentioned in SCS 3.1.1. This lease could *possibly* fall outside the warranty because it is within SCS 3.1.2 (b) as discoverable by inspection, or, in a very odd case but not here, SCS 3.1.2 (c) as something the seller does not and could not know about. But we will assume that in this case it is within the warranty. This means, as has been discussed above, that the buyer can sue on the warranty for title after completion (see SCS 7.4). So a problem for the buyer arises only if SCS 7.4 does not apply to this contract or if the contractual warranty in SCS 3 has not been given. Equally the buyer will have a remedy if there has been misrepresentation or deliberate concealment. If none of these apply then we must fall back on the covenant for title. The property in question is the field purported to be transferred to Mr East. The s. 3 covenant (read with r. 77A) is to the effect that those fields are free from any third-party right except for entries on the register and overriding interests of which the buyer has notice. Notice will arise, for example, if Mr West is in possession of the land; but if notice is not present Mr East will have his remedy on the covenant for title.

Lesser registered titles

There may also be scope for the covenants for title in registered land to operate in respect of unregistered parts of the title purported to be conveyed. Generally the covenant given in s. 2 is restricted to the title actually registered — see s. 2(2)(a) covenanting that the seller will do 'all that he reasonably can to ensure that the person to whom the disposition is made is entitled to be registered as proprietor with at least the class of title registered immediately before the disposition'. If under

44

the contract the seller is to transfer a larger title than the registered then the s. 2 covenant will be accordingly enlarged in scope.

The s. 3 covenant (freedom from encumbrances) will in the same way apply to the title purported to be conveyed.

Where a seller purports to sell a larger title than that with which he is registered the contract will make this clear. The presumption given by s. 3(3)(a) may assist the seller to avoid inadvertently contracting to sell a title greater than the registered title. It provides that where the sale is of a registered title then subject to the terms of the instrument, 'where the title to the interest is registered, it shall be presumed that the disposition is of the whole of that interest'.

Variation of covenants registered land

It should be noted that rule 77A(3) provides that where a covenant implied by a section of the new act is limited or extended then that section should be expressly referred to in the instrument. This wording does not negate the effect of express covenants which operate independently of the new Act (for a contrary view see Sol Jo 1995 p. 508).

Covenants for title and particular conveyancing parties

A sole beneficial owner

In the pre-1995 regime a sole beneficial owner gave the beneficial owner covenant without any great pause for thought. The new full title guarantee is undoubtedly materially more onerous in the following significant ways:

(a)   The seller can be liable for a encumbrance or defect in title created by a predecessor through whom the seller claims for value. This was not so under the pre-1995 law (see, e.g., *David* v *Sabin* [1893] 1 Ch 523).

(b)   The obligation to make good the title is at the expense of the covenantor. The obligation also obliges the covenantor to take the necessary steps to ensure registration in the Land Registry.

In their practical effect these do not add up to sufficient reason to refuse to follow the intended purpose of the legislation and replace the beneficial owner covenant with the full title guarantee.

A sole surviving joint tenant

Under the old law a sole surviving joint tenant would give the beneficial owner covenant and in future will give a full title guarantee. There is an amendment to the Law of Property (Joint Tenants) Act 1964, s. 1(1), which should be noted. Paragraph 3 of sch. 1 to the 1994 Act removes the words 'he conveys as beneficial owner or' from the section.

The 1964 Act was passed to remedy a lacuna in the 1925 property legislation. How was a purchaser from a sole surviving joint tenant to know that the seller was entitled to convey as sole beneficial owner and did not have to appoint a second trustee to ensure that any beneficial interests under the trust for sale would be overreached? The difficulty was that the beneficial joint tenancy could have been severed before the death of the other beneficial owner. The 1964 Act provides that in the specified circumstances it can be assumed that the sole survivor is beneficially entitled if he conveys as beneficial owner or the conveyance includes a statement that he is so interested. In future, no one (except in transitional cases) will convey as beneficial owner so in future a conveyance by a sole surviving joint tenant will contain an appropriate recital or statement that he is solely and beneficially entitled. See appendix 1 No. 12.

Joint beneficial owners

Under the pre-1995 law one of the most pointless yet frequent disputes between conveyancers was whether joint beneficial owners should give the beneficial owner or the trustee covenant. The clearly correct view was that where the parties were in fact the beneficial owners that was the correct covenant to give and would be the one to which the court would undoubtedly (if the question ever arose) have given effect. In future joint beneficial owners should convey with full title guarantee as should sole beneficial owners.

Trustees for sale, personal representative, mortgagee, tenant for life

In pre-1995 conveyancing these parties gave the limited owner covenant set out in Part II of sch. 2 to the Law of Property Act 1925. The clear purpose of the 1994 Act is that they should in future give a limited title guarantee. There is no reason in future why such parties should not give that guarantee. It is materially different from the former limited owner covenant in the following ways:

(a)   The covenant in s. 2(1) of the 1994 Act that the covenantor has the right to convey is an addition to the former covenant and so is the covenant for further assurance in s. 2(2).

(b)   The covenant that the covenantor has not charged or encumbered the property or suffered it to be charged or encumbered etc. is wider than that given under the old law. In particular there is the addition 'that he is not aware that anyone else has done so since the last disposition for value' (s. 3(3)). Aldridge (*Implied Covenant for Title — Conveyancers' Handy Guide*) makes this important comment:

> Where property is sold by trustees who are themselves successors to the trustees who originally acquired it, it may be argued that they are 'aware' of matters which were brought to their predecessors' attention even though they have no personal knowledge of them.

The covenant can be limited to exclude such deemed knowledge. It is the writer's view that this is unnecessarily cautious. 'Aware', as has been already discussed, is a word which describes a conscious state of mind not one imputed to a person. So the primary meanings given in the *Shorter Oxford English Dictionary* are 'Watchful, on one's guard, informed, cognisant, conscious, sensible'. No amendment to the covenant is therefore necessary because of the concern expressed by Aldridge. However, for the hypercautious, No. 15 in appendix 1 is a suitable amendment.

Conveyance by a donor or settlor

Under the pre-1995 practice a covenant for title was implied where a person conveyed as settlor — see the Law of Property Act 1925, s. 76, and sch. 2, part V. This was a covenant for further assurance at the cost of the person deriving the title. Under the new law there is no equivalent of this covenant. A donor or settlor will give no covenant for title at all. This is perfectly reasonable as 'no one looks a gift horse in the mouth'. Very rare cases occur where a settlement is bargained for — in the past this would be 'upon the treaty for a marriage' where the agreement would be given effect to in a marriage settlement. In such a case, where value is thought to be given, the parties might conclude that the statutory covenants for title should be given by the use of the appropriate words.

On an assent or vesting assent

There is no reason in this case why the personal representative, should give any covenant for title at all. They are not bound in law to do so and shoud be advised not to incur for themselves or the estate this potential liability.

A sale by a receiver or trustee in bankruptcy

A receiver should give a limited title guarantee. See the comment on mortgagees above. This is an area where truculent argument is particularly likely. Buyers should point out to the seller that the transaction is an arm's-length sale. Why should a buyer be denied the promise in s. 2 that the seller has the right to sell what is purported to be sold? So far as the promise in s. 3 of freedom from encumbrances is covered, the limited promise in s. 3(3) is not unduly onerous as explained above (page 19). The receiver or trustee is in a position to know whether he or she has encumbered the property or suffered it to be encumbered — for the rest a receiver is liable only for matters of which he or she is aware.

Covenants for title under particular statutes

Section 21 and sch. 1 make provision for there to be specified covenants for title implied under certain Acts of Parliament.

Under the Leasehold Reform Act 1967 on enfranchisement

Section 10 the Leasehold Reform Act 1967 is amended by para. 5 of sch. 1 to the 1994 Act. The effect of the amendment is that the landlord may be required to convey with limited title guarantee. The landlord is, though, entitled to be reimbursed by the tenant for any costs incurred in complying with s. 2(1)(b) of this 1994 Act — that is, for doing what it can to give the title it purports to give. This last is subject to any agreement to the contrary, though it is improbable that there will ever be such an agreement.

Under the Leasehold Reform Act 1967 on grant of an extended lease

Section 15 of the Leasehold Reform Act 1967 is amended by para. 5(2) of sch. 1 to the 1994 Act. The effect is that the landlord gives any covenant implied from the grant and a limited title guarantee. This covenant does not include the promise in s. 4(1)(b) that there is no subsisting breach of the tenant's obligations in the lease and nothing which would render the lease liable to forfeiture. Unless there is agreement to the contrary, the implied covenant entitled the landlord to be reimbursed in respect of any costs incurred in complying with s. 2(1)(b) of the 1994 Act — that is, the covenant for further assurance. Section 15(9A) of the 1967 Act provides that the landlord is entitled to limit personal liability under the covenant to breaches of the covenant for which the landlord is responsible.

Under the Rentcharges Act 1967

Few rentcharges will have been created after 22 August 1977 when the Rentcharges Act 1977 came into force. Section 2(3) of that Act specifies the circumstances in which rentcharges can still be created. Two of these circumstances are a rentcharge:

    (a)   which has the effect of making the land on which the rent is charged settled land by virtue of section 1(1)(v) of the Settled Land Act 1925:

    (b)   which would have that effect but for the fact that the land on which the rent is charged is already settled land or is held on trust for sale.

In these two cases, s. 11 of the Rentcharges Act 1977 specified the covenant for title to be given on a sale of the land subject to the rentcharge. That provision continues to apply to dispositions of such land after the 1994 Act comes into force except that it is amended by sch. 1, para. 5(3). The section as amended and as it was before amendment is set out in appendix 1 below.

Under the Housing Act 1985

This is amended so that the landlord is required to convey the freehold or grant a 'right to buy' a lease with full title guarantee.

Leasehold Reform, Housing and Urban Development Act 1993

A number of amendments to this Act are made by para. 12 of sch. 1 to the 1994 Act. The result is as follows. The landlord is bound to give a title with limited title guarantee on enfranchisement. The freeholder is entitled to be repaid by the nominee purchaser for any cost there is of complying with s. 2(1)(b) of the 1994 Act — the covenant for further assurance. On the grant of a new lease, the landlord is required to give any covenant implied from the grant and a limited title guarantee and to be repaid any cost there is of complying with s. 2(1)(b) of the 1994 Act — the covenant for further assurance.

Where there is a grant of a lease back to the former leaseholder under sch. 9 to the 1993 Act then the covenants to be given are those implied from the grant and the limited title guarantee (1994 Act, sch. 1, para. 12(4)).

4

Remedies for Breach of Covenants for Title

Specific performance

The covenant contained in s. 2 of the 1994 Act (right to dispose and further assurance) is clearly one in respect of which an action for specific performance can be maintained. The various parts of the covenant are matters in respect of which an order for specific performance can be sought. Difficulties will arise, not in principle with the remedy of specific performance, but in practice in framing the order and selecting the appropriate party against whom an order should be made.

Where A has granted a lease to B there may be a defect in A's title because A is a tenant for life who has exceeded his statutory power of leasing. B may assign this lease to C before the matter is discovered. If title guarantees have been given in each case then C may have an action on the covenant for title against both A and B. An order that each of A and B will do all they reasonably can at their own expense to remedy this defect is hardly worth having unless either A or B is in a position actually to remedy the defect. This is very likely to require the concurrence of other persons interested in the settled estate against whom, of course, no order for specific performance can be made.

Damages

Where the seller has not complied with the covenant in s. 2 then the prima facia measure of damages will be no different from under the previous law. This will be the difference in value between that purported to be conveyed and that actually conveyed — see, e.g., *Turner* v *Moon* [1901] 2 Ch 825.

An important question is the date of measuring the damages. *Barnsley's Conveyancing Law and Practice*, 3rd ed. (London: Butterworths, 1988) says simply that this is at the date of the conveyance (p. 604). This view is not in conformity with modern principles of contract law which will doubtless apply in assessing damages under these provisions. The modern rule is made clear by the House of Lords in *Johnson* v *Agnew* [1980] AC 367 at p. 401 and is that damages are normally assessed at the date of the breach, but where this would give rise to injustice, the court has power to fix such other date as may be appropriate in the circumstances.

Where the seller is in breach of the covenant implied by s. 3 the same basic measure of damages will be available by reference to a sum payable to remove an encumbrance. This may be recoverable as such — see *Great Western Railway Co.* v *Fisher* [1905] 1 Ch 316. In other cases this may be assessable by reference to a reduction in value of the land as a result of the existence of the encumbrance — see, e.g., *Sutton* v *Baillie* (1891) 65 LT 528.

Particular nineteenth-century decisions in this area should not be regarded as definitive. The question is one of breach of contract where the principles for assessment have not remained unchanged.

Self-help

The possibility of self-help should not be overlooked in dealing with a churlish vendor. The purchaser may put the defect right and then recover the proper costs and expenses incurred in doing so from the vendor who has failed to put right the defect personally. Notice should be given to the seller who is delaying or refusing to take the necessary steps that this course of action will be followed if the matter is not dealt with within a specified reasonable time. This will be important in resisting an argument that the expenditure is more than is reasonable in the circumstances. If this course of action is followed the expenditure can be recovered by a simple action in the county court.

Limitation

The period of limitation in respect of breach of a covenant for title is 12 years (Limitation Act 1980, s. 8). This does not apply as such to a claim for specific performance (Limitation Act 1980, s. 36). The 12-year period may be extended in a variety of circumstances (see the Limitation Act 1980, part II; Latent Damage Act 1986).

Time runs from the breach. In the case of the covenant that the seller has a good title there is a breach on execution of the relevant deed (see *Spoor* v *Green* (1874) LR 9 Ex 99; *Turner* v *Moon* [1901] 2 Ch 825). In the former case this was expressed by Bramwell B as, 'The covenant remains broken indeed, but broken once, for all'. This has been the subject of controversy, the contrary argument being that the failure to make a good title is a continuing breach. Where the covenant requires the seller to take steps to make good the title (further assurance) there is a breach when the seller fails to do so (see *Spoor* v *Green* at p. 110).

So far as the covenant in s. 3 of the 1994 Act is concerned this seems to fall within the first rule — that the seller is in breach at the time of the conveyance. This view is strengthened by the fact that the new covenants contain no covenant for quiet enjoyment — this latter is broken at the time of the relevant act (see *Spoor* v *Green* and *Turner* v *Moon*, particularly the explanation by Joyce J in the latter).

Appendix 1

Suggested Clauses

Type of document	*Form of words*
1 An unregistered conveyance — to introduce covenants for title.	conveys with full title guarantee to the purchaser
	conveys with limited title guarantee to the purchaser
2 A transfer under r. 72 of the Land Registration Rules 1925 — to introduce covenants for title.	[the transferor] transfers the land with full title guarantee to ...
	[the transferor] transfers the land with limited title guarantee to ...
3 A transfer of registered land — to introduce covenants for title.	[the transferor] transfers the land in the above title with full title guarantee to ...
	[the transferor] transfers the land in the above title with limited title guarantee to ...
4 In the grant of a lease — to introduce covenants for title.	The landlord grants ... with full title guarantee.
	The landlord grants ... with limited title guarantee.

5   A mortgage or charge — to introduce covenants for title.

[The mortgagor] with full title guarantee hereby charges by way of legal mortgage. [See the Law of Property Act 1925, sch. 4, Form No. 1.]

6   A transfer of a mortgage — to introduce covenants for title.

[The mortgagee] with full [or limited] title guarantee hereby transfers to [transferee]. [See the Law of Property Act 1925, sch. 4, Form No. 2.]

7   A further charge — to introduce covenants for title.

As for 3 above. [See the Law of Property Act 1925, sch. 5, Form No. 2.]

8   A conveyance in which the mortgagee concurs — to introduce covenants for title.

The seller with full [or limited] title guarantee conveys and the mortgagee (with limited title guarantee) releases to the purchaser .... [See the Law of Property Act 1925, sch. 5, Form No. 3.]

9   A conveyance by a legal mortgagee — to introduce the covenants for title.

The seller with limited [or full] title guarantee and in exercise of the power conferred by the Law of Property Act 1925, and of all other powers, hereby conveys .... [See the Law of Property Act 1925, sch. 5, Form No. 4.]

10   An assent — to introduce the covenants for title. Ordinarily, it is suggested, no covenant will be given.

[The personal representatives] with limited title guarantee assent etc. [See the Law of Property Act 1925, sch. 5, Form Nos. 8 and 9.]

11   In a surrender — to introduce covenants for title.

[The tenant] with full [or limited] title guarantee surrenders ....

12   On a sale of unregistered land by a sole surviving joint tenant to gain

The seller declares that he [she] is solely beneficially entitled to the

55

the benefit of the Law of Property (Joint Tenants) Act 1964. (This is unnecessary in the case of registered land, see s. 2 of the 1964 Act.)

land and with full title guarantee conveys . . . .

13   Provision to make the conveyance subject to a specified matter

[The property is transferred] subject to [and then set out clearly the nature of the particular encumbrance].

14   Provision to throw the cost of compliance with the covenant for further assurance in s. 2(1)(b) upon the covenantee

With full title guarantee but so that section 2(1)(b) of the Law of Property (Miscellaneous Provisions) Act 1994 reads as if the words 'at his own cost' are replaced by the words 'at the cost of the covenantee'.

15   Provision to vary the limited title guarantee to apply only to acts or omissions of the covenantor (not those of which the covenantor is aware).

With limited title guarantee but so that in section 3(3) of the Law of Property (Miscellaneous Provisions) Act 1994 the words from 'and that he is not aware' to the end inclusive are omitted.

16   On the sale of a lease — to give the covenant for title but exclude any promise that there is no breach of the lease (with a variation to limit this exception to 'repair' covenants).

With full title guarantee [or limited title guarantee] but so that the covenantor is not liable for any subsisting breach of a term of the lease [or of a term of the lease relating to the condition of the property].

17   On the sale of an underlease — to give the covenant for title but exclude any promise that there is no breach of a condition in the head lease.

With full title guarantee [or limited title guarantee] but so that there is no liability for a subsisting breach of any term of [specify the relevant head lease].

18   Provision in a disposition to ensure that the pre-1995 covenants are implied in a post-Act disposition

This [conveyance/transfer] is made pursuant to a contract . . . day of . . . which provided for the seller where s. 11 (the transitional provisions) applies. See page 30 above.

to convey as [insert as the case may be].

19   Provisions in a disposition of a registered leasehold interest made pursuant to a pre-Act contract to ensure that the pre-Act covenants are implied when s. 11 (the transitional provision) applies. See page 30 above.

This transfer is made pursuant to a contract made the ... day of....

20   To vary the Standard Conditions of Sale on the grant of a long lease so that the purchaser is entitled only to good leasehold title, i.e., the reversionary title is not be deduced.

SCS 8.2.4 does not apply and the covenant for title given extends only to the buyer being registered with good leasehold title.

Appendix 2

Text of the Law of Property (Miscellaneous Provisions) Act 1994

1994 CHAPTER 36

An Act to provide for new covenants for title to be implied on dispositions of property; to amend the law with respect to certain matters arising in connection with the death of the owner of property; and for connected purposes.

[3rd November 1994]

Be it enacted by the Queen's most Excellent Majesty, by and with the advice and consent of the Lords Spiritual and Temporal, and Commons, in this present Parliament assembled, and by the authority of the same, as follows:—

PART I   IMPLIED COVENANTS FOR TITLE

The covenants

1.   Covenants to be implied on a disposition of property

(1)   In an instrument effecting or purporting to effect a disposition of property there shall be implied on the part of the person making the disposition, whether or not the disposition is for valuable consideration, such of the covenants specified in sections 2 to 5 as are applicable to the disposition.

(2)   Of those sections—

(a)   sections 2, 3(1) and (2), 4 and 5 apply where dispositions are expressed to be made with full title guarantee; and

(b)   sections 2, 3(3), 4 and 5 apply where dispositions are expressed to be made with limited title guarantee.

(3)   Sections 2 to 4 have effect subject to section 6 (no liability under covenants in certain cases); and sections 2 to 5 have effect subject to section

8(1) (limitation or extension of covenants by instrument effecting the disposition).

(4) In this Part—

'disposition' includes the creation of a term of years;

'instrument' includes an instrument which is not a deed; and

'property' includes a thing in action, and any interest in real or personal property.

2. Right to dispose and further assurance

(1) If the disposition is expressed to be made with full title guarantee or with limited title guarantee there shall be implied the following covenants—

(a) that the person making the disposition has the right (with the concurrence of any other person conveying the property) to dispose of the property as he purports to, and

(b) that that person will at his own cost do all that he reasonably can to give the person to whom he disposes of the property the title he purports to give.

(2) The latter obligation includes—

(a) in relation to a disposition of an interest in land the title to which is registered, doing all that he reasonably can to ensure that the person to whom the disposition is made is entitled to be registered as proprietor with at least the class of title registered immediately before the disposition; and

(b) in relation to a disposition of an interest in land the title to which is required to be registered by virtue of the disposition, giving all reasonable assistance fully to establish to the satisfaction of the Chief Land Registrar the right of the person to whom the disposition is made to registration as proprietor.

(3) In the case of a disposition of an existing legal interest in land, the following presumptions apply, subject to the terms of the instrument, in ascertaining for the purposes of the covenants implied by this section what the person making the disposition purports to dispose of—

(a) where the title to the interest is registered, it shall be presumed that the disposition is of the whole of that interest;

(b) where the title to the interest is not registered, then—

(i) if it appears from the instrument that the interest is a leasehold interest, it shall be presumed that the disposition is of the property for the unexpired portion of the term of years created by the lease; and

(ii) in any other case, it shall be presumed that what is disposed of is the fee simple.

3. Charges, incumbrances and third party rights

(1) If the disposition is expressed to be made with full title guarantee there shall be implied a covenant that the person making the disposition is disposing of the property free—

    (a)   from all charges and incumbrances (whether monetary or not), and

    (b)   from all other rights exercisable by third parties,

other than any charges, incumbrances or rights which that person does not and could not reasonably be expected to know about.

    (2)   In its application to charges, incumbrances and other third party rights subsection (1) extends to liabilities imposed and rights conferred by or under any enactment, except to the extent that such liabilities and rights are, by reason of—

    (a)   being, at the time of the disposition, only potential liabilities and rights in relation to the property, or

    (b)   being liabilities and rights imposed or conferred in relation to property generally,

not such as to constitute defects in title.

    (3)   If the disposition is expressed to be made with limited title guarantee there shall be implied a covenant that the person making the disposition has not since the last disposition for value—

    (a)   charged or incumbered the property by means of any charge or incumbrance which subsists at the time when the disposition is made, or granted third party rights in relation to the property which so subsists, or

    (b)   suffered the property to be so charged or incumbered or subjected to any such rights,

and that he is not aware that anyone else has done so since the last disposition for value.

4. Validity of lease

    (1)   Where the disposition is of leasehold land and is expressed to be made with full title guarantee or with limited title guarantee, the following covenants shall also be implied—

    (a)   that the lease is subsisting at the time of the disposition, and

    (b)   that there is no subsisting breach of a condition or tenant's obligation, and nothing which at that time would render the lease liable to forfeiture.

    (2)   If the disposition is the grant of an underlease, the references to 'the lease' in subsection (1) are references to the lease out of which the underlease is created.

5. Discharge of obligations where property subject to rentcharge or leasehold land

    (1)   Where the disposition is a mortgage of property subject to a rentcharge, or of leasehold land, and is expressed to be made with full title guarantee or with limited title guarantee, the following covenants shall also be implied.

(2) If the property is subject to a rentcharge, there shall be implied a covenant that the mortgagor will fully and promptly observe and perform all the obligations under the instrument creating the rentcharge that are for the time being enforceable with respect to the property by the owner of the rentcharge in his capacity as such.

(3) If the property is leasehold land, there shall be implied a covenant that the mortgagor will fully and promptly observe and perform all the obligations under the lease subject to the mortgage that are for the time being imposed on him in his capacity as tenant under the lease.

(4) In this section 'mortgage' includes charge, and 'mortgagor' shall be construed accordingly.

Effect of covenants

6. No liability under covenants in certain cases

(1) The person making the disposition is not liable under the covenants implied by virtue of—

  (a) section 2(1)(a) (right to dispose),

  (b) section 3 (charges, incumbrances and third party rights), or

  (c) section 4 (validity of lease),

in respect of any particular matter to which the disposition is expressly made subject.

(2) Furthermore that person is not liable under any of those covenants for anything (not falling within subsection (1))—

  (a) which at the time of the disposition is within the actual knowledge, or

  (b) which is a necessary consequence of facts that are then within the actual knowledge,

of the person to whom the disposition is made.

(3) For this purpose section 198 of the Law of Property Act 1925 (deemed notice by virtue of registration) shall be disregarded.

7. Annexation of benefit of covenants

The benefit of a covenant implied by virtue of this Part shall be annexed and incident to, and shall go with, the estate or interest of the person to whom the disposition is made, and shall be capable of being enforced by every person in whom that estate or interest is (in whole or in part) for the time being vested.

8. Supplementary provisions

(1) The operation of any covenant implied in an instrument by virtue of this Part may be limited or extended by a term of that instrument.

(2) Sections 81 and 83 of the Law of Property Act 1925 (effect of covenant with two or more jointly; construction of implied covenants) apply to a

covenant implied by virtue of this Part as they apply to a covenant implied by virtue of that Act.

(3)   Where in an instrument effecting or purporting to effect a disposition of property a person is expressed to direct the disposition, this Part applies to him as if he were the person making the disposition.

(4)   This Part has effect—

(a)   where 'gyda gwarant teitl llawn' is used instead of 'with full title guarantee', and

(b)   where 'gyda gwarant teitl cyfyngedig' is used instead of 'with limited title guarantee',

as it has effect where the English words are used.

9.   Modifications of statutory forms

(1)   Where a form set out in an enactment, or in an instrument made under an enactment, includes words which (in an appropriate case) would have resulted in the implication of a covenant by virtue of section 76 of the Law of Property Act 1925, the form shall be taken to authorise instead the use of the words 'with full title guarantee' or 'with limited title guarantee' or their Welsh equivalent given in section 8(4).

(2)   This applies in particular to the forms set out in Schedule 1 to the Settled Land Act 1925 and Schedules 4 and 5 to the Law of Property Act 1925.

Transitional provisions

10.   General saving for covenants in old form

(1)   Except as provided by section 11 below (cases in which covenants in old form implied on disposition after commencement), the following provisions, namely—

(a)   section 76 of the Law of Property Act 1925, and

(b)   section 24(1)(a) of the Land Registration Act 1925,

are repealed as regards dispositions of property made after the commencement of this Part.

(2)   The repeal of those provisions by this Act accordingly does not affect the enforcement of a covenant implied by virtue of either of them on a disposition before the commencement of this part.

11.   Covenants in old form implied in certain cases

(1)   Section 76 of the Law of Property Act 1925 applies in relation to a disposition of property made after the commencement of this Part in pursuance of a contract entered into before commencement where—

(a)   the contract contains a term providing for a disposition to which that section would have applied if the disposition had been made before commencement, and

(b)   the existence of the contract and of that term is apparent on the face of the instrument effecting the disposition,

unless there has been an intervening disposition of the property expressed, in accordance with this Part, to be made with full title guarantee.

(2)   Section 24(1)(a) of the Land Registration Act 1925 applies in relation to a disposition of a leasehold interest in land made after the commencement of this Part in pursuance of a contract entered into before commencement where—

(a)   the covenant specified in that provision would have been implied on the disposition if it had been made before commencement, and

(b)   the existence of the contract is apparent on the face of the instrument effecting the disposition,

unless there has been an intervening disposition of the leasehold interest expressed, in accordance with this Part, to be made with full title guarantee.

(3)   In subsections (1) and (2) an 'intervening disposition' means a disposition after the commencement of this Part to, or to a predecessor in title of, the person by whom the disposition in question is made.

(4)   Where in order for subsection (1) or (2) to apply it is necessary for certain matters to be apparent on the face of the instrument effecting the disposition, the contract shall be deemed to contain an implied term that they should so appear.

12.   Covenants in new form to be implied in other cases

(1)   This section applies to a contract for the disposition of property entered into before the commencement of this Part where the disposition is made after commencement and section 11 (cases in which covenants in old form to be implied) does not apply because there has been an intervening disposition expressed, in accordance with this Part, to be with full title guarantee.

(2)   A contract which contains a term that the person making the disposition shall do so as beneficial owner shall be construed as requiring that person to do so by an instrument expressed to be made with full title guarantee.

(3)   A contract which contains a term that the person making the disposition shall do so—

(a)   as settlor, or

(b)   as trustee or mortgagee or personal representative,

shall be construed as requiring that person to do so by an instrument expressed to be made with limited title guarantee.

(4)   A contract for the disposition of a leasehold interest in land entered into at a date when the title to the leasehold interest was registered shall be construed as requiring the person making the disposition for which it provides to do so by an instrument expressed to be made with full title guarantee.

(5)   Where this section applies and the contract provides that any of the covenants to be implied by virtue of section 76 of the Law of Property Act 1925 or section 24(1)(a) of the Land Registration Act 1925 shall be implied in a modified form, the contract shall be construed as requiring a corresponding modification of the covenants implied by virtue of this Part.

13.   Application of transitional provisions in relation to options

For the purposes of sections 11 and 12 (transitional provisions, implication of covenants in old form in certain cases and new form in others) as they apply in relation to a disposition of property in accordance with an option granted before the commencement of this Part and exercised after commencement, the contract for the disposition shall be deemed to have been entered into on the grant of the option.

PART II   MATTERS ARISING IN CONNECTION WITH DEATH

14.   Vesting of estate in case of intestacy or lack of executors

(1)   For section 9 of the Administration of Estates Act 1925 (vesting of estate of intestate between death and grant of administration) substitute—

'9.   Vesting of estate in Public Trustee where intestacy or lack of executors

(1)   Where a person dies intestate, his real and personal estate shall vest in the Public Trustee until the grant of administration.

(2)   Where a testator dies and—

(a)   at the time of his death there is no executor with power to obtain probate of the will, or

(b)   at any time before probate of the will is granted there ceases to be any executor with power to obtain probate,

the real and personal estate of which he disposes by the will shall vest in the Public Trustee until the grant of representation.

(3)   The vesting of real or personal estate in the Public Trustee by virtue of this section does not confer on him any beneficial interest in, or impose on him any duty, obligation or liability in respect of, the property.'

(2)   Any real or personal estate of a person dying before the commencement of this section shall, if it is property to which this subsection applies, vest in the Public Trustee on the commencement of this section.

(3)   Subsection (2) above applies to any property—

(a)   if it was vested in the Probate Judge under section 9 of the Administration of Estates Act 1925 immediately before the commencement of this section, or

(b)   if it was not so vested but as at commencement there has been no grant of representation in respect of it and there is no executor with power to obtain such a grant.

(4)   Any property vesting in the Public Trustee by virtue of subsection (2) above shall—

(a)   if the deceased died intestate, be treated as vesting in the Public Trustee under section 9(1) of the Administration of Estates Act 1925 (as substituted by subsection (1) above); and

(b)   otherwise be treated as vesting in the Public Trustee under section 9(2) of that Act (as so substituted).

(5)   Anything done by or in relation to the Probate Judge with respect to property vested in him as mentioned in subsection (3)(a) above shall be treated as having been done by or in relation to the Public Trustee.

(6)   So far as may be necessary in consequence of the transfer to the Public Trustee of the functions of the Probate Judge under section 9 of the Administration of Estates Act 1925, any reference in an enactment or instrument to the Probate Judge shall be construed as a reference to the Public Trustee.

15.   Registration of land charges after death

(1)   The Land Charges Act 1972 is amended as follows.

(2)   In section 3 (registration of land charges), after subsection (1) (registration in name of estate owner), insert—

'(1A)   Where a person has died and a land charge created before his death would apart from his death have been registered in his name, it shall be so registered notwithstanding his death.'

(3)   In section 5 (register of pending actions), after subsection (4) (entry in name of person whose estate or interest is intended to be affected), insert—

'(4A)   Where a person has died and a pending land action would apart from his death have been registered in his name, it shall be so registered notwithstanding his death.'

(4)   In section 6 (register of writs and orders affecting land), after subsection (2) (entry in name of estate owner or other person whose land is affected), insert—

'(2A)   Where a person has died and any such writ or order as is mentioned in subsection (1)(a) or (b) above would apart from his death have been registerd in his name, it shall be so registered notwithstanding his death.'

(5)   The amendments made by this section do not apply where the application for registration was made before the commencement of this section,

but without prejudice to a person's right to make a new application after commencement.

16. Concurrence of personal representatives in dealings with interests in land

(1)   In section 2(2) of the Administration of Estates Act 1925 (concurrence of all personal representatives required for conveyance of real estate)—

(a)   after 'a conveyance of real estate devolving under this Part of this Act' insert 'or a contract for such a conveyance';

(b)   omit the words ', save as otherwise provided as respects trust estates including settled land,' (which are unnecessary); and

(c)   after 'any conveyance of the real estate' insert 'or contract for such a conveyance'.

(2)   Section 2(2) of the Administration of Estates Act 1925 as amended by subsection (1) above (concurrence of all personal represenatives required for conveyance of real estate or contract for such conveyance) applies in relation to an interest under a trust for sale of land as in relation to real estate.

(3)   The amendments made by subsection (1) apply to contracts made after the commencement of this section; and subsection (2) applies to contracts made after the commencement of this section and to conveyances so made otherwise than in pursuance of a contract made before commencement.

17. Notices affecting land: absence of knowledge of intended recipient's death

(1)   Service of a notice affecting land which would be effective but for the death of the intended recipient is effective despite his death if the person serving the notice has no reason to believe that he has died.

(2)   Where the person serving a notice affecting land has no reason to believe that the intended recipient has died, the proper address for the purposes of section 7 of the Interpretation Act 1978 (service of documents by post) shall be what would be the proper address apart from his death.

(3)   The above provisions do not apply to a notice authorised or required to be served for the purposes of proceedings before—

(a)   any court,

(b)   any tribunal specified in Schedule 1 to the Tribunals and Inquiries Act 1992 (tribunals within general supervising of Council on Tribunals), or

(c)   the Chief Land Registrar or any district registrar or assistant district registrar;

but this is without prejudice to the power to make provision in relation to such proceedings by rules of court, procedural rules within the meaning of section

8 of the Tribunals and Inquiries Act 1992 or rules under section 144 of the Land Registration Act 1925.

18. Notices affecting land, service on personal representatives before filing of grant

(1) A notice affecting land which would have been authorised or required to be served on a person but for his death shall be sufficiently served before a grant of representation has been filed if—

(a) it is addressed to 'The Personal Representatives of' the deceased (naming him) and left at or sent by post to his last known place of residence or business in the United Kingdom, and

(b) a copy of it, similarly addressed, is served on the Public Trustee.

(2) The reference in subsection (1) to the filing of a grant of representation is to the filing at the Principal Registry of the Family Division of the High Court of a copy of a grant of representation in respect of the deceased's estate or, as the case may be, the part of his estate which includes the land in question.

(3) The method of service provided for by this section is not available where provision is made—

(a) by or under any enactment, or

(b) by an agreement in writing,

requiring a different method of service, or expressly prohibiting the method of service provided for by this section, in the circumstances.

19. Functions of Public Trustee in relation to notices, etc.

(1) The Public Trustee may give directions as to the office or offices at which documents may be served on him—

(a) by virtue of section 9 of the Administration of Estates Act 1925 (as substituted by section 14(1) above), or

(b) in pursuance of section 18(1)(b) above (service on Public Trustee of copy of certain notices affecting land);

and he shall publish such directions in such manner as he considers appropriate.

(2) The Lord Chancellor may by regulations make provision with respect to the functions of the Public Trustee in relation to such documents; and the regulations may make different provision in relation to different descriptions of document or different circumstances.

(3) The regulations may, in particular, make provision requiring the Public Trustee—

(a) to keep such documents for a specified period and thereafter to keep a copy or record of their contents in such form as may be specified;

(b) to keep such documents, copies and records available for inspection at such reasonable hours as may be specified; and

(c) to supply copies to any person on request.

In this subsection 'specified' means specified by or under the regulations.

(4)   Regulations under this section shall be made by statutory instrument which shall be subject to annulment in pursuance of a resolution of either House of Parliament.

(5)   The following provisions of the Public Trustee Act 1906, namely—

(a)   section 8(5) (payment of expenses out of money provided by Parliament), and

(b)   section 9(1), (3) and (4) (provisions as to fees),

apply in relation to the functions of the Public Trustee in relation to documents to which this section applies as in relation to his functions under that Act.

PART III   GENERAL PROVISIONS

20.   Crown application

This Act binds the Crown.

21.   Consequential amendments and repeals

(1)   The enactments specified in Schedule 1 are amended in accordance with that Schedule, the amendments being consequential on the provisions of this Act.

(2)   The enactments specified in Schedule 2 are repealed to the extent specified.

(3)   In the case of section 76 of the Law of Property Act 1925 and section 24(1)(a) of the Land Registration Act 1925, those provisions are repealed in accordance with section 10(1) above (general saving for covenants in old form).

(4)   The amendments consequential on Part I of this Act (namely those in paragraphs 1, 2, 3, 5, 7, 9 and 12 of Schedule 1) shall not have effect in relation to any disposition of property to which, by virtue of section 10(1) or 11 above (transitional provisions), section 76 of the Law of Property Act 1925 or section 24(1)(a) of the Land Registration Act 1925 continues to apply.

22.   Extent

(1)   The provisions of this Act extend to England and Wales.

(2)   In addition—

(a)   the provisions of Schedules 1 and 2 (consequential amendments and repeals) extend to Scotland so far as they relate to enactments which so extend; and

(b)   the provisions of Schedule 1 extend to Northern Ireland so far as they relate to enactments which so extend.

23.   Commencement

(1)   The provisions of this Act come into force on such day as the Lord Chancellor may appoint by order made by statutory instrument.

(2)   Different days may be appointed for different provisions and for different purposes.

24.   Short title

This Act may be cited as the Law of Property (Miscellaneous Provisions) Act 1994.

SCHEDULE 1   CONSEQUENTIAL AMENDMENTS

Law of Property Act 1925 (c. 20)

1.   In section 77(1) of the Law of Property Act 1925 (implied covenants in conveyances subject to rents), for 'the last preceding section' substitute 'Part I of the Law of Property (Miscellaneous Provisions) Act 1994'.

Land Registration Act 1925 (c. 21)

2.   In section 38(2) of the Land Registration Act 1925 (effect of implied covenants in dispositions of registered land), after 'the Law of Property Act 1925' insert 'or Part I of the Law of Property (Miscellaneous Provisions) Act 1994'.

Law of Property (Joint Tenants) Act 1964 (c. 63)

3.   In section 1(1) of the Law of Property (Joint Tenants) Act 1964 (assumptions on sale of land by survivor of joint tenants), omit the words 'he conveys as beneficial owner or'.

Land Commission Act 1967 (c. 1)

4.—(1)   In Part II of Schedule 12 to the Land Commission Act 1967 (betterment levy: effect of death etc. on liability), paragraph 10 (provisions as to intestacy) is amended as follows.

(2)   In sub-paragraph (1)—

(a)   for 'the Probate Judge', in each place where the words occur, substitute 'the Public Trustee'; and

(b)   for 'letters of administration of that person's estate are granted' substitute 'a grant of representation is made in respect of that person's estate'.

(3)   Omit sub-paragraph (2) (definition of 'the Probate Judge').

Leasehold Reform Act 1967 (c. 88)

5.—(1)   In section 10 of the Leasehold Reform Act 1967 (rights to be conveyed to tenant on enfranchisement), in subsection (1) omit the words from 'nor to enter into any covenant for title' to the end, and after that subsection insert—

'(1A)   The landlord shall not be required to enter into any covenant for title beyond those implied under Part I of the Law of Property (Miscellaneous Provisions) Act 1994 in a case where a disposition is expressed to be made with limited title guarantee; and in the absence of agreement to the contrary he shall be entitled to be indemnified by the tenant in respect of any costs incurred by him in complying with the covenant implied by virtue of section 2(1)(b) of that Act (covenant for further assurance).'

(2)   In section 15 of that Act (terms of tenancy to be granted on extension, for subsection (9) substitute—

'(9)   In granting the new tenancy, the landlord shall not be bound to enter into any covenant for title beyond—

(a)   those implied from the grant, and

(b)   those implied under Part I of the Law of Property (Miscellaneous Provisions) Act 1994 in a case where a disposition is expressed to be made with limited title guarantee, but not including (in the case of a sub-tenancy) the covenant in section 4(1)(b) of that Act (compliance with terms of lease); and in the absence of agreement to the contrary the landlord shall be entitled to be indemnified by the tenant in respect of any costs incurred by him in complying with the covenant implied by virtue of section 2(1)(b) of that Act (covenant for further assurance).

(9A)   A person entering into any covenant required of him as landlord (under subsection (9) or otherwise) shall be entitled to limit his personal liability to breaches of that covenant for which he is responsible.'

(3)   In Schedule 1 to that Act (enfranchisement or extension by sub-tenants), in paragraph 7(1)(a), after 'that tenancy' insert ', and the reference in subsection (1A) of that section to the covenants for title implied under Part I of the Law of Property (Miscellaneous Provisions) Act 1994 shall be read as excluding the covenant in section 4(1)(b) of that Act (compliance with terms of lease)'.

Consumer Credit Act 1974 (c. 39)

6.   In section 176 of the Consumer Credit Act 1974 (service of documents), for subsection (7) (service not to be effected on Probate Judge) substitute—

'(7)   The following enactments shall not be construed as authorising service on the Public Trustee (in England and Wales) or the Probate Judge (in Northern Ireland) of any document which is to be served under this Act—

section 9 of the Administration of Estates Act 1925;

section 3 of the Administration of Estates Act (Northern Ireland) 1955.'

Rentcharges Act 1977 (c. 30)

7. In section 11(2) of the Rentcharges Act 1977 (additional covenants relating to rentcharge deemed included and implied in conveyance), for 'section 76 of the Law of Property Act 1925' substitute 'Part I of the Law of Property (Miscellaneous Provisions) Act 1994'.

Rent Act 1977 (c. 42)

8. In Part I of Schedule 2 to the Rent Act 1977 (provisions for determining application of resident landlord exemption), in paragraph 1 (periods to be disregarded in ascertaining whether landlord resident at all times since grant of tenancy), in sub-paragraph (c)(iii) (period during which interest of landlord vested in Probate Judge), for 'the Probate Judge, within the meaning of that Act' substitute 'the Probate Judge or the Public Trustee'.

Housing Act 1985 (c. 68)

9.—(1) Schedule 6 to the Housing Act 1985 (conveyance of freehold or grant of lease in pursuance of right to buy) is amended as follows.

(2) In Part I (common provisions), after paragraph 4 insert—

'4A. The conveyance or grant shall be expressed to be made by the landlord with full title guarantee (thereby implying the covenants for title specified in Part I of the Law of Property (Miscellaneous Provisions) Act 1994).'

(3) In paragraph 5, for 'covenants' substitute 'other covenants'.

(4) In Part II (conveyance of freehold), omit paragraph 10.

Financial Services Act 1986 (c. 60)

10. In section 45(1) of the Financial Services Act 1986 (miscellaneous exemptions from regulation of investment business), in paragraph (a) for 'the President of the Family Division of the High Court' substitute 'the Public Trustee'.

Housing Act 1988 (c. 50)

11. In Part III of Schedule 1 to the Housing Act 1988 (provisions for determining application of resident landlord exemption), in paragraph 17 (periods to be disregarded in ascertaining whether landlord resident at all times since grant of tenancy), in sub-paragraph (c)(ii) (period during which interest of landlord vested in Probate Judge), for 'the Probate Judge, within the meaning of that Act' substitute 'the Probate Judge or the Public Trustee'.

Leasehold Reform, Housing and Urban Development Act 1993 (c. 28)

12.—(1)   In section 34 of the Leasehold Reform, Housing and Urban Development Act 1993 (conveyance to nominee purchaser), in subsection (9) after second 'conveyed' add ', and with the reference to the covenants for title implied under Part I of the Law of Property (Miscellaneous Provisions) Act 1994 being read as excluding the covenant in section 4(1)(b) of that Act (compliance with terms of lease)'.

(2)   In section 57 of that Act (terms on which new lease is to be granted), for subsection (8) substitute—

'(8)   In granting the new lease the landlord shall not be bound to enter into any covenant for title beyond—

(a)   those implied from the grant, and

(b)   those implied under Part I of the Law of Property (Miscellaneous Provisions) Act 1994 in a case where a disposition is expressed to be made with limited title guarantee, but not including (in the case of an underlease) the covenant in section 4(1)(b) of that Act (compliance with terms of lease);

and in the absence of agreement to the contrary the landlord shall be entitled to be indemnified by the tenant in respect of any costs incurred by him in complying with the covenant implied by virtue of section 2(1)(b) of that Act (covenant for further assurance).

(8A)   A person entering into any covenant required of him as landlord (under subsection (8) or otherwise) shall be entitled to limit his personal liability to breaches of that covenant for which he is responsible.'

(3)   In Schedule 7 to the Act (conveyance to nominee purchaser on enfranchisement), for paragraph 2(2)(b) substitute—

'(b)   to enter into any covenant for title beyond those implied under Part I of the Law of Property (Miscellaneous Provisions) Act 1994 in a case where a disposition is expressed to be made with limited title guarantee;

and in the absence of agreement to the contrary the freeholder shall be entitled to be indemnified by the nominee purchaser in repect of any costs incurred by him in complying with the covenant implied by virtue of section 2(1)(b) of that Act (covenant for further assurance).'

(4)   In Schedule 9 to that Act (grant of leases back to former freeholder) after paragraph 9 insert—

'Covenants for title

9A.   The lessor shall not be bound to enter into any covenant for title beyond—

(a)   those implied from the grant, and

(b)   those implied under Part I of the Law of Property (Miscellaneous Provisions) Act 1994 in a case where a disposition is expressed to be made with limited title guarantee.'

SCHEDULE 2   REPEALS

Chapter	Short title	Extent of repeal
15 & 16 Geo. 5 c. 20.	Law of Property Act 1925.	Section 76. In Schedule 2, Parts I to VI.
15 & 16 Geo. 5 c. 21.	Land Registration Act 1925.	Section 24(1)(a).
15 & 16 Geo. 5 c. 23.	Administration of Estates Act 1925.	In section 2(2), the words ", save as otherwise provided as respects trust estates including settled land," Section 36(3). In section 55(1), paragraph (xv).
1964 c. 63.	Law of Property (Joint Tenants) Act 1964.	In section 1(1), the words "he conveys as beneficial owner or".
1967 c. 1.	Land Commission Act 1967.	In Schedule 12, paragraph 10(2).
1967 c. 88.	Leasehold Reform Act 1967.	In section 10(1), from the words "nor to enter into any covenant for title" to the end.
1970 c. 31.	Administration of Justice Act 1970.	In Schedule 2, paragraph 5.
1985 c. 6.	Companies Act 1985.	Section 209(10)(d).
1985 c. 68.	Housing Act 1985.	In Schedule 6, paragraph 10.

Appendix 3

Text of the Law of Property Act 1925, Schedule 2

SCHEDULE 2   IMPLIED COVENANTS

PART I   COVENANT IMPLIED IN A CONVEYANCE FOR VALUABLE CONSIDERATION, OTHER THAN A MORTGAGE, BY A PERSON WHO CONVEYS AND IS EXPRESSED TO CONVEY AS BENEFICIAL OWNER

That, notwithstanding anything by the person who so conveys or any one through whom he derives title otherwise than by purchase for value, made, done, executed, or omitted, or knowingly suffered, the person who so conveys has, with the concurrence of every other person, if any, conveying by his direction, full power to convey the subject-matter expressed to be conveyed, subject as, if so expressed, and in the manner in which, it is expressed to be conveyed, and that, notwithstanding anything as aforesaid, that subject-matter shall remain to and be quietly entered upon, received, and held, occupied, enjoyed, and taken, by the person to whom the conveyance is expressed to be made, and any person deriving title under him, and the benefit thereof shall be received and taken accordingly, without any lawful interruption or disturbance by the person who so conveys or any person conveying by his direction, or rightfully claiming or to claim by, through, under, or in trust for the person who so conveys, or any person conveying by his direction, or by, through, or under any one (not being a person claiming in respect of an estate or interest subject whereto the conveyance is expressly made), through whom the person who so conveys derives title, otherwise than by purchase for value:

And that, freed and discharged from, or otherwise by the person who so conveys sufficiently indemnified against, all such estates, incumbrances, claims and demands, other than those subject to which the conveyance is expressly made, as, either before or after the date of the conveyance, have been or shall be made, occasioned, or suffered by that person or by any person conveying by his direction, or by any person rightfully claiming by, through, under, or in trust for the person who so conveys, or by, through, or under any person conveying by his direction, by, through, or under any one through whom the person who so conveys derives title, otherwise than by purchase for value.

And further, that the person who so conveys, and any person conveying by his direction, and every other person having or rightfully claiming any estate or interest in the subject-matter of conveyance, other than an estate or interest subject whereto the conveyance is expressly made, by, through, under, or in trust for the person who so conveys, or by, through, or under any person conveying by his direction, or by, through, or under any one through whom the person who so conveys derives title, otherwise than by purchase for value, will from time to time and at all times after the date of the conveyance, on the request and at the cost of any person to whom the conveyance is expressed to be made, or of any person deriving title under him, execute and do all such lawful assurances and things for further or more perfectly assuring the subject-matter of the conveyance to the person to whom the conveyance is made, and to those deriving title under him, subject as, if so expressed, and in the manner in which the conveyance is expressed to be made, as by him or them or any of them shall be reasonably required.

In the above covenant a purchase for value shall not be deemed to include a conveyance in consideration of marriage.

PART II   FURTHER COVENANT IMPLIED IN A CONVEYANCE OF LEASEHOLD PROPERTY FOR VALUABLE CONSIDERATION, OTHER THAN A MORTGAGE, BY A PERSON WHO CONVEYS AND IS EXPRESSED TO CONVEY AS BENEFICIAL OWNER

That, notwithstanding anything by the person who so conveys, or any one through whom he derives title, otherwise than by purchase for value, made, done, executed, or omitted, or knowingly suffered, the lease or grant creating the term or estate for which the land is conveyed is, at the time of conveyance, a good, valid, and effectual lease or grant of the property conveyed, and is in full force, unforfeited, unsurrendered, and has in nowise become void or voidable, and that, notwithstanding anything as aforesaid, all the rents reserved by, and all the covenants, conditions, and agreements contained in, the lease or grant, and on the part of the lessee or grantee and the persons deriving title under him to be paid, observed, and performed, have been paid, observed, and performed up to the time of conveyance.

In the above covenant a purchase for value shall not be deemed to include a conveyance in consideration of marriage.

PART III   COVENANT IMPLIED IN A CONVEYANCE BY WAY OF MORTGAGE BY A PERSON WHO CONVEYS AND IS EXPRESSED TO CONVEY AS BENEFICIAL OWNER

That the person who so conveys, has, with the concurrence of every other person, if any, conveying by his direction, full power to convey the subject-matter expressed to be conveyed by him, subject as, if so expressed, and in the manner in which it is expressed to be conveyed:

And also that, if default is made in payment of the money intended to be secured by the conveyance, or any interest thereon, or any part of that money or interest, contrary to any provision in the conveyance, it shall be lawful for the person to whom the conveyance is expressed to be made, and the persons deriving title under him, to enter into and upon, or receive, and thenceforth quietly hold, occupy, and enjoy or take and have, the subject-matter expressed to be conveyed, or any part thereof, without any lawful interruption or disturbance by the person who so conveys, or any person conveying by his direction, or any other person (not being a person claiming in respect of an estate or interest subject whereto the conveyance is expressly made):

And that, freed and discharged from, or otherwise by the person who so conveys sufficiently indemnified against all estates, incumbrances, claims, and demands whatever, other than those subject whereto the conveyance is expressly made:

And further, that the person who so conveys and every person conveying by his direction, and every person deriving title under any of them, and every other person having or rightfully claiming any estate or interest in the subject-matter of conveyance, or any part thereof, other than an estate or interest subject whereto the conveyance is expressly made, will from time to time and at all times, on the request of any person to whom the conveyance is expressed to be made, or of any person deriving title under him, but, as long as any right of redemption exists under the conveyance, at the cost of the person so conveying, or of those deriving title under him, and afterwards at the cost of the person making the request, execute and do all such lawful assurances and things for further or more perfectly assuring the subject-matter of conveyance and every part thereof to the person to whom the conveyance is made, and to those deriving title under him, subject as, if so expressed, and in the manner in which the conveyance is expressed to be made, as by him or them or any of them shall be reasonably required.

The above covenant in the case of a charge shall have effect as if for references be 'conveys', 'conveyed' and 'conveyance' there were substituted respectively references to 'charges', charged' and 'charge'.

PART IV   COVENANT IMPLIED IN A CONVEYANCE BY WAY OF MORTGAGE OF FREEHOLD PROPERTY SUBJECT TO A RENT OR OF LEASEHOLD PROPERTY BY A PERSON WHO CONVEYS AND IS EXPRESSED TO CONVEY AS BENEFICIAL OWNER

That the lease or grant creating the term or estate for which the land is held is, at the time of conveyance, a good, valid, and effectual lease or grant of the land conveyed and is in full force, unforfeited, and unsurrendered and has in nowise become void or voidable, and that all the rents reserved by, and all the covenants, conditions, and agreements contained in, the lease or grant, and on the part of the lessee or grantee and the persons deriving title under him to be paid, observed, and performed, have been paid, observed, and performed up to the time of conveyance:

And also that the person so conveying, or the persons deriving title under him, will at all times, as long as any money remains owing on the security of the conveyance, pay, observe, and perform, or cause to be paid, observed, and performed all the rents reserved by, and all the covenants, conditions, and agreements contained in, the lease or grant, and on the part of the lessee or grantee and the persons deriving title under him to be paid, observed, and performed, and will keep the person to whom the conveyance is made, and those deriving title under him, indemnified against all actions, proceedings, costs, charges, damages, claims and demands, if any, to be incurred or sustained by him or them by reason of the non-payment of such rent or the non-observance or non-performance of such covenants, conditions, and agreements, or any of them.

The above covenant in the case of a charge shall have effect as if for references be 'conveys', 'conveyed' and 'conveyance' there were substituted respectively references to 'charges', charged' and 'charge'.

PART V   COVENANT IMPLIED IN A CONVEYANCE BY WAY OF SETTLEMENT, BY A PERSON WHO CONVEYS AND IS EXPRESSED TO CONVEY AS SETTLOR

That the person so conveying, and every person deriving title under him by deed or act or operation of law in his lifetime subsequent to that conveyance, or by testamentary disposition or devolution in law, on his death, will, from time to time, and at all times, after the date of that conveyance, at the request and cost of any person deriving title thereunder, execute and do all such lawful assurances and things for further or more perfectly assuring the subject-matter of the conveyance to the persons to whom the conveyance is made and those deriving title under them, as by them or any of them shall be reasonably required, subject as, if so expressed, and in the manner in which the conveyance is expressed to be made.

PART VI COVENANT IMPLIED IN ANY CONVEYANCE, BY EVERY PERSON WHO CONVEYS AND IS EXPRESSED TO CONVEY AS TRUSTEE OR MORTGAGEE, OR AS PERSONAL REPRESENTATIVE OF A DECEASED PERSON, OR UNDER AN ORDER OF THE COURT

That the person so conveying has not executed or done, or knowingly suffered, or been party or privy to, any deed or thing, whereby or by means whereof the subject-matter of the conveyance, or any part thereof, is or may be impeached, charged, affected, or incumbered in title, estate, or otherwise, or whereby or by means whereof the person who so conveys is in anywise hindered from conveying the subject-matter of the conveyance, or any part thereof, in the manner in which it is expressed to be conveyed.

The foregoing covenant may be implied in an assent in like manner as in a conveyance by deed.

PART VII COVENANT IMPLIED IN A CONVEYANCE FOR VALUABLE CONSIDERATION, OTHER THAN A MORTGAGE, OF THE ENTIRETY OF LAND AFFECTED BY A RENTCHARGE

That the grantees or the persons deriving title under them will at all times, from the date of the conveyance or other date therein stated, duly pay the said rentcharge and observe and perform all the covenants, agreements and conditions contained in the deed or other document creating the rentcharge, and thenceforth on the part of the owner of the land to be observed and performed:

And also will at all times, from the date aforesaid, save harmless and keep indemnified the conveying parties and their respective estates and effects, from and against all proceedings, costs, claims and expenses on account of any omission to pay the said rentcharge or any part thereof, or any breach of any of the said covenants, agreements and conditions.

PART VIII COVENANTS IMPLIED IN A CONVEYANCE FOR VALUABLE CONSIDERATION, OTHER THAN A MORTGAGE, OF PART OF LAND AFFECTED BY A RENTCHARGE, SUBJECT TO A PART (NOT LEGALLY APPORTIONED) OF THAT RENTCHARGE

(i)   That the grantees, or the persons deriving title under them, will at all times, from the date of the conveyance or other date therein stated, pay the apportioned rent and observe and perform all the covenants (other than the covenant to pay the entire rent) and conditions contained in the deed or other document creating the rentcharge, so far as the same relate to the land conveyed:

And also will at all times, from the date aforesaid, save harmless and keep indemnified the conveying parties and their respective estates and effects, from and against all proceedings, cost, claims and expenses on account of any omission to pay the said apportioned rent, or any breach of any of the said covenants and conditions, so far as the same relate as aforesaid.

(ii)   That the conveying parties, or the persons deriving title under them, will at all times, from the date of the conveyance or other date therein stated, pay the balance of the rentcharge (after deducting the apportioned rent aforesaid, and any other rents similarly apportioned in respect of land not retained), and observe and perform all the covenants, other than the covenant to pay the entire rent, and conditions contained in the deed or other document creating the rentcharge, so far as the same relate to the land not included in the conveyance and remaining vested in the covenantors:

And also will at times, from the date aforesaid, save harmless and keep indemnified the grantees and their estates and effects, from and against all proceedings, costs, claims and expenses on account of any omission to pay the aforesaid balance of the rentcharge, or any breach of any of the said covenants and conditions so far as they relate as aforesaid.

PART IX COVENANT IN A CONVEYANCE FOR VALUABLE CONSIDERATION, OTHER THAN A MORTGAGE, OF THE ENTIRETY OF THE LAND COMPRISED IN A LEASE FOR THE RESIDUE OF THE TERM OR INTEREST CREATED BY THE LEASE

That the assignees, or the persons deriving title under them, will at all times, from the date of the conveyance or other date therein stated, duly pay all rent becoming due under the lease creating the term or interest for which the land is conveyed, and observe and perform all the covenants, agreements and conditions therein contained and thenceforth on the part of the lessees to be observed and performed:

And also will at all times, from the date aforesaid, save harmless and keep indemnified the conveying parties and their estates and effects, from and against any proceedings, costs, claims and expenses on account of any omission to pay the said rent or any breach of any of the said covenants, agreements and conditions.

PART X   COVENANT IMPLIED IN A CONVEYANCE FOR VALUABLE CONSIDERATION, OTHER THAN A MORTGAGE, OR PART OF THE LAND COMPRISED IN A LEASE, FOR THE RESIDUE OF THE TERM OR INTEREST CREATED BY THE LEASE, SUBJECT TO A PART (NOT LEGALLY APPORTIONED) OF THE RENT

(i)   That the assignees, or the persons deriving title under them, will at all times, from the date of the conveyance or other date therein stated, pay the apportioned rent and observe and perform all the covenants, other than the covenant to pay the entire rent, agreements and conditions contained in the lease creating the term or interest for which the land is conveyed, and thenceforth on the part of the lessees to be observed and performed, so far as the same relate to the land conveyed:

And also will at all times from the date aforesaid save harmless and keep indemnified, the conveying parties and their respective estates and effects, from and against all proceedings, costs, claims and expenses on account of any omission to pay the said apportioned rent or any breach of any of the said covenants, agreements and conditions so far as the same relate as aforesaid.

(ii)   That the conveying parties, or the persons deriving title under them, will at all times, from the date of the conveyance, or other date therein stated, pay the balance of the rent (after deducting the apportioned rent aforesaid and any other rents similarly apportioned in respect of land not retained) and observe and perform all the covenants, other than the covenant to pay the entire rent, agreements and conditions contained in the lease and on the part of the lessees to be observed and performed so far as the same relate to the land demised (other than the land comprised in the conveyance) and remaining vested in the covenantors:

And also will at all times, from the date aforesaid, save harmless and keep indemnified, the assignees and their estates and effects, from and against all proceedings, costs, claims and expenses on account of any omission to pay the aforesaid balance of the rent or any breach of any of the said covenants, agreements and conditions so far as they relate as aforesaid.

Appendix 4

Text of the Land Registration Act 1925, Section 38

38. Certain provisions of the Law of Property Act to apply

(1) The provisions as to execution of a conveyance on sale contained in the Law of Property Act 1925 shall apply, so far as applicable thereto, to transfers on sale of registered land,

(2) Rules may be made for prescribing the effect of covenants implied by virtue of the Law of Property Act 1925 in dispositions of registered land.

Appendix 5

Text of the Land Registration Rules 1925, Rules 76 and 77 as Originally Made

76. Implied covenants

For the purpose of introducing the covenants implied under sections 76 and 77 of the Law of Property Act 1925 a person may, in a registered disposition, be expressed to execute, transfer, or charge as beneficial owner, as settlor, as trustee, as mortgagee, as personal representative of a deceased person, as committee of a lunatic, or as receiver of a defective, or under an order of the court: and an instrument of transfer or charge, and any instrument affecting registered land, or a registered charge, may be expressed accordingly, but no reference to covenants implied under section 76 aforesaid shall be entered in the register.

77. Special provisions as to implied covenants

Pursuant to subsection (2) of section 38 of the Act, it is hereby provided that—

(1) Any covenant implied by virtue of section 76 of the Law of Property Act 1925 in a disposition of registered land shall take effect as through the disposition was expressly made subject to—

(a) all charges and other interests appearing or protected on the register at the time of the execution of the disposition and affecting the title of the covenantor;

(b) any overriding interests of which the purchaser has notice and subject to which it would have taken effect, had the land been unregistered; and

(2) The benefit of an covenant implied under sections 76 and 77 aforesaid, or either of them shall, on and after the registration of the disposition in which it is implied, be annexed and incident to and shall go with the registered proprietorship of the interest for the benefit of which it is given and shall be capable of being enforced by the proprietor for the time being thereof.

(3)   The provisions of this rule are in addition to and not in substitution for the other provisions relating to covenants contained in the said Act.

(4)   Provided that where covenants are to be implied under section 77 aforesaid, with or without modification, express reference shall be made in the disposition to that section or to the Parts of the 2nd Schedule to that Act in which the covenants are set out.

Appendix 6

Text of the Land Registration (Implied Covenants for Title) Rules 1995

SI 1995/377

Made	*15th February 1995*
Laid before Parliament	*17th February 1995*
Coming into force	*1st July 1995*

The Lord Chancellor, with the advice and assistance of the Rule Committee appointed in pursuance of section 144 of the Land Registration Act 1925, in exercise of the powers conferred on him by that section and by section 38(2) of that Act, hereby makes the following rules:

Citation, commencement and interpretation

1.—(1) These rules may be cited as the Land Registration (Implied Covenants for Title) Rules 1995 and shall come into force on 1st July 1995.

(2) In these rules a rule referred to by number means the rule so numbered in the Land Registration Rules 1925.

New rule 76

2. The following rule shall be substituted for rule 76:

'**Covenants implied under section 77 of the Law of Property Act 1925**

76. For the purpose of introducing the covenants implied under paragraphs (B)(ii) and (D)(ii) of section 77(1) of the Law of Property Act 1925 a person may, in a registered disposition:

(a) be expressed to execute, transfer or charge as beneficial owner; or

(b) where the instrument effecting the disposition expressly refers to section 77 of the Law of Property Act 1925, be expressed to execute, transfer or charge as settlor, trustee, mortgagee, or personal representative of a deceased person, or under an order of the court, and the instrument effecting the disposition may be framed accordingly.'.

New rule 76A

3. The following rule shall be inserted after rule 76:

'**Covenants implied under Part I of the Law of Property (Miscellaneous Provisions) Act 1994**

76A.—(1) In this rule 'the 1994 Act' means the Law of Property (Miscellaneous Provisions) Act 1994.

(2) Subject to paragraph (3), a registered disposition may be expressed to be made either with full title guarantee or with limited title guarantee and, in the case of a disposition which is effected by an instrument in the Welsh language, the appropriate Welsh expression specified in section 8(4) of the 1994 Act may be used.

(3) In the case of a registered disposition to which section 76 of the Law of Property Act 1925 applies by virtue of section 11(1) of the 1994 Act, a person may be expressed to execute, transfer or charge as beneficial owner, settlor, trustee, mortgagee, or personal representative of a deceased person or under an order of the court, and the instrument effecting the disposition may be framed accordingly.

(4) Except as provided in paragraph (5), no reference to any covenant implied by virtue of Part I of the 1994 Act, or by section 76 of the Law of Property Act 1925 as applied by section 11(1) of the 1994 Act, shall be made in the register.

(5) A reference may be made in the register where a registered disposition of leasehold land limits or extends the covenant implied under section 4 of the 1994 Act.'.

Amendment to rule 77

4. Rule 77 shall be amended as follows:

(a) the words 'pursuant to subsection (2) of section 38 of the Act, it is hereby provided that—' shall be deleted;

(b) in paragraph (1), for the words 'Any covenant' there shall be substituted the words 'In relation to a disposition of registered land to which section 76 of the Law of Property Act 1925 applies by virtue of section 11(1) of the Law of Property (Miscellaneous Provisions) Act 1994, any covenant';

(c) in paragraph (1), for the words 'a disposition of registered land' there shall be substituted the words 'such a disposition';

(d) in paragraph (2), for the word 'aforesaid' there shall be substituted the words 'of the Law of Property Act 1925';

(e) paragraph (4) shall be deleted.

85

New rule 77A

5. The following rule shall be inserted after rule 77:

'**Additional provisions as to implied covenants**

77A.—(1) In this rule 'the 1994 Act' means the Law of Property (Miscellaneous Provisions) Act 1994.

(2) Any covenant implied by virtue of Part I of the 1994 Act in a registered disposition shall take effect as if the disposition had been expressly made subject to:—

(a) all charges and other interests appearing or protected on the register at the time of the execution of the disposition and affecting the title of the registered proprietor;

(b) any overriding interest of which the person to whom the disposition is made has notice and which will affect the estate created or disposed of when the disposition is registered.

(3) Where the instrument effecting a registered disposition contains a provision limiting or extending any covenant implied by virtue of Part I of the 1994 Act express reference shall be made to the section of that Act in which the covenant is set out.'.

Amendment to rule 115

6. In rule 115(2) the words 'or by Part I of the Law of Property (Miscellaneous Provisions) Act 1994,' shall be inserted after the words 'section 24,'.

Amendment to rule 117

7. In rule 117 the words 'or Part I of the Law of Property (Miscellaneous Provisions) Act 1994,' shall be inserted after the words 'Law of Property Act 1925,'.

15th February 1995   *Mackay of Clashfern,* C

Index

Index

Freedom from encumbrances
— *continued*
limited title guarantee   19–21
registered land   42, 43, 45
scope of covenant   20–1
Standard Conditions of Sale   34
Full title guarantee   3
freedom from encumbrances   15–19
seller unwilling to give   33–4
in Welsh   28
Further assurance   8–9, 11–12
cost to seller   11–12
further evidence of title required
12
obligation to assist with registration
12–13
reasonableness   11–12

Gas companies   15
Gift   12
Good right to convey   9–10
Grant of lease   21–3
extended lease   49
landlord right   22

Housing Act 1985   4, 50

Inspection of property   38
Instrument
disposition effected by   6–7
rectification   14
requirements   7
subject to terms of   14
variations expressly referred to in   45
Intervening dispositions   32

Knowledge of buyer   25–6, 38

Land, covenants run with   3, 40
Land Registration Act 1925   41
section 38 text   81
Land Registration (Implied Covenants for
Title) Rules 1995, text   84–6
Land Registration Rules 1925   41
Rules 76 and 77 text   82–3
Landlords
under Housing Act 1985   4, 50
under Leasehold Reform Act 1967
4, 49

Landlords — *continued*
under Leasehold Reform, Housing and
Urban Development Act 1993
4, 50
Last disposition for value   19
Law Commission
reasons for reform   2
*Transfer of Land: Implied Covenants
for Title*   1
Law of Property Act 1925, Schedule 2
text   74–80
Law of Property (Miscellaneous
Provisions) Act 1994, text   58–73
Lay persons, comprehensibility of law
for   2–3
Leasehold land
assignment of lease consent   11
enfranchisement   49, 50
freedom from encumbrances   22–3
grant of lease   21–3
extended lease   49
landlord right   22
leaseback   50
mortgage   23–4
no subsisting breach of term   23
rack rent   22
rentcharge   23–4
Standard Conditions of Sale   35
Leasehold Reform Act 1967   4, 49
Leasehold Reform, Housing and Urban
Development Act 1993   4, 50
Licences grant   8
Limitation for breach of covenant for
title   53
Limited title guarantee   3
freedom from encumbrances
19–21
Listed building orders   18

Merger doctrine   35, 36
Misrepresentation   2
rescission for   39
Mistake, rescission for   38–9
Mortgage, on leasehold land   23–4
Mortgagees   47
benefit of previous covenants
40–1
covenants in mortgage   39–40
sale by   12, 40–1

88

244355

COVENANTS FOR TITLE:

UNDERSTANDING THE NEW LAW

Professor Phillip H. Kenny

The new Law of Property (Miscellaneous Provisions) Act 1994 Part I that came into force on 1 July 1995 impacts upon every single conveyancing transaction. In future sellers will have the option to sell with "Full Title Guarantee" or with "Limited Title Guarantee" and these guarantees potentially impose heavy financial burdens upon the seller. With the increased risk involved in conveyancing it is essential that all solicitors involved in property be aware of the impact of this Act and reconsider their office precedents accordingly.

This important new title provides a practical guide to the Act and shows how to use the covenants for title. It includes a section by section commentary of the new Act, together with an account of the complicated transitional arrangements, with tables to illustrate the changes.

This will be essential reading for all licensed conveyancers and solicitors practising in this field. It will also be of interest to mortgage industry professionals.

The book contains a copy of the Act.

Contents Include: The Basic Scheme; The Legislation Described; Practical Use of the Covenant for Title; Remedies; Suggested Clauses; Law of Property (Miscellaneous Provisions) Act 1994; Other Legislation.

About the Author: Professor Phillip H. Kenny is Head of the School of Law at the University of Northumbria and Consultant to Messrs. Dickinson Dees, Solicitors. He is the author of various books on conveyancing, property law and other topics, and has much experience in all aspects of conveyancing and conveyancing-related litigation.

ISBN 1-85431-471-8

£12.95 net in UK

9 781854 314710